FAMILY DEVOTIONAL BUILDER

Devotional Resources
for Elementary Age Children
and Their Parents

Karen H. Whiting

Illustrated by Eira Reeves

HENDRICKSON
PUBLISHERS

Hendrickson Publishers, Inc.
P.O. Box 3473
Peabody
Massachusetts 01961-3473
USA

ISBN 1-56563-567-1

Designed by
ANDREW MILNE DESIGN

Original edition published in English under the title
Family Devotional Builder by John Hunt Publishing Ltd.

Write to John Hunt Publishing Ltd
46a West Street, Alresford, Hampshire SO24 9AU, UK

Printed in Singapore

If you have health problems, consult your physician before participating
in any of the physical activities in the book.

DEDICATION

*Dedicated to my husband Jim and our five children: Rebecca, Michael, James,
Darlene, and Daniel; for their support, love, and endurance as they enjoyed the
blessings of God and sharing together through these activities.*

CONTENTS

Discovering Talents

Happy is the family that knows children are full of potential for they will develop their talents!

God made each person unique with special qualities and talents. Discovering abilities and talents is a lifetime treasure hunt! Use these activities to excite children in discovering their potential!

— MATERIALS —

✧ envelopes — 1 per person
✧ small objects from around the house (elastics, cotton balls, coins, bandage, stickers, paper clips, etc.)
✧ cardboard
✧ glue and tape
✧ crayons or pencils — one per person

NOTE: This is one of the few devotions needing advance preparation.

 Preparation

Before the family gathers, cut cardboard slightly smaller than the envelopes and attach random office and household items to the cardboard. Then place the cardboard inside an envelope and seal it. Attempt to have each envelope contain a different combination of items with at least 3 items on each cardboard. Written words dealing with talents can be included. Make 1 envelope per person.

DAY 1

SEALED TREASURES

PSALM 139:1-2 *O Lord, you have searched me and you know me. You know when I sit and when I rise; you perceive my thoughts from afar.*

 Activity

Each person takes an envelope and writes their own name on it. Keep the envelopes closed. Let everyone feel their envelope. Can they guess any of the contents just by touching?

 Talk about it

How does God give us special talents? We are still discovering our abilities. Some of the contents of the envelope can be discovered by touch. Some people know their gifts and talents easily in life – such as singing, sports ability and natural beauty! Let each person talk about one talent they know God gave them! What talents did a parent first notice in each child! When did they discover it?

DAY 2

RUBBING UP ANSWERS

PSALM 139:13-14 *For you created my inmost being; you knit me together in my mother's womb. I praise you because I am fearfully and wonderfully made; your works are wonderful, I know that full well.*

 Activity

Pass out pencils or crayons and use them to rub across the envelopes revealing more about the contents.

 Talk about it

Some things were revealed by rubbing. Some abilities are discovered when people do things with one another – such as a talent of encouraging others, counseling, or problem solving. Parents, tell each child one hidden talent you have seen in them when they are with other people.

DAY 3

REVEALED ANSWERS

ROMANS 12:6 *We have different gifts, according to the grace given us...*

 Activity

Open the envelopes and look inside!

 Talk about it

Some things were only revealed by opening up the envelope. Some people's talents are not known until God opens their lives and reveals them. We are different and we each have distinct gifts and talents. Ask God to reveal your gifts and talents and help you to use them wisely! Take time to pray for God's wisdom.

 Deeper exploration

Talk about the contents and how the items can be used. For example a coin can be saved, spent, tossed, used as a game marker, given away, or used for bribery. Talents can be used for good or evil. God gives us the talents but we choose how to use them.

Let everyone list the talents they notice in themselves and see if someone else observes other talents to add to the list. Discuss how creativity adds sparkle to these talents and how these talents can be used.

Cups of Blessings

Happy is the family that gives thanks
for they will be richly blessed!

Enjoy learning with cup puppets and overflowing cups!

— MATERIALS —

- ✧ *2 white paper or Styrofoam cups per person*
- ✧ *1 paper fastener for each person*
- ✧ *markers*
- ✧ *scissors*
- ✧ *glue*
- ✧ *brown, red, and black construction paper*
- ✧ *shallow pan*
- ✧ *clear glass*
- ✧ *large container (pitcher size) and spoon or tiny glass*
- ✧ *optional: flex straws, black pompoms*

DAY 1

MAKE PAPER CUP DOG PUPPETS

NEHEMIAH 1:11...*I was the cupbearer to the King.*

Activity

As cup bearer for King Artaxerxes, Nehemiah tasted the King's drink, making sure it was safe. Use cup puppets as cup bearers to talk about our King!

Talk about it

These cups took on a whole new look by adding a few things! Likewise, we become new in Christ with God's word and love.

Directions

1. Put one cup upside down on a table. This is the puppet body.

2. Turn the other cup on its side so it is perpendicular to the first cup. This is the puppet head. The bottom of this cup is used for the head of the puppet.

3. Place the head on top of the body. Set the "head cup" further forward on the bottom cup for a longer snout. The head can be cut shorter if desired.

4. Put a paper fastener through the 2 cups passing through the center of the bottom cup. Now the head can turn and one hand can be put in the body to hold the puppet. A flex straw can be used as a rod by taping the straw inside the opening of the puppet's head to turn the puppets head.

5. Draw eyes. Add paper ears and tongue and a paper or pompom nose.

6. Add a tail and paper paws to the cup body.

DAY 2

PERFORMING

MARK 7:28 *"Yes Lord," she replied, "but even the dogs under the table eat the children's crumbs."*

 Activity

Perform the dog skit based on *Mark 7:24-30* with the dog puppets.

 Talk about it

Are you happy with what God gives?

DAY 3

CUPS OVERFLOWING WITH BLESSINGS!

PSALM 23:5 *You prepare a table before me in the presence of my enemies. You anoint my head with oil, my cup overflows.*

 Activity

Let your cups overflow with thanks in this activity: Set an empty cup inside a shallow dish or pan. Fill a large container with water. Let each person fill the spoon or tiny glass with water and pour it into the cup in the pan while telling one thing for which they thank God. Keep going around until the cup overflows! Go one more round letting each person overflow the cup.

 Talk about it

How does it help to thank God?

 Dog Script

SCAMP Ruff, ruff. I had a really interesting time. I followed a crowd. Thought maybe someone would give me a snack or scratch me behind my ears.

PETE A crowd? Too dangerous for me. Probably had to put up with getting your tail pulled and being kicked around.

SCAMP Not this time. Everyone was busy following a special man.

PETE Not a dog catcher, I hope!

SCAMP Nope. His name is Jesus.

PETE I've heard of Him. The miracle worker.

SCAMP That's the one. He was talking to a Gentile woman.

PETE Uh-oh that might be the end for Him. Jewish leaders call that a no-no!!

SCAMP He told her she couldn't eat the children's bread – that it was not right to give it to a dog! I wasn't too happy to hear He wouldn't feed dogs!

PETE Guess He's not much of a dog lover!

SCAMP Well, then she said that dogs were allowed to eat scraps from the table. I figured she was a kind soul so I started to follow her.

PETE Always going after the best meal giver!

SCAMP Well, He agreed with her then and there. He told her she had great faith and He healed her daughter. That got me to thinking…

PETE Now that is mind-boggling. Amazing that you would think instead of following your nose!

SCAMP Well, it made me decide to follow this Jesus and find out more!!

Bread Plates

*Happy is the family that knows God must be visible in
our lives for others will see Christ through them!*

U se these activities as a reminder
of the presence of Jesus, the bread
of life.

— MATERIALS —

✧ *paper plate*
✧ *crayons and pencils*
✧ *slips of paper*
✧ *clear contact paper (optional)*
✧ *bread*

DAY 1

MAKE A BREAD PLATE!

MATTHEW 18:20 *For where two or three come
together in my name, there am I with them.*

 Activity

Take a paper plate and draw a design on it that
pictures bread or Jesus as the Bread of Life.
Write your names. Color the plate. Cover it with
clear contact paper (or make a more permanent
plate with a solid colored plastic plate and
permanent markers).

Use the plate at meal times to hold bread,
crackers, rolls, or bread slices. At each meal,
place the bread plate in front of the family
member who will lead the prayer of grace for
that meal. After grace, that family member can
break the bread and pass it to others.

When you have company, use the bread plate to
share Jesus, the bread of life, with your guests!!
Let your children explain why you use a bread
plate!

 Talk about it

Jesus, the Bread of Life, is always with us and we
need him daily! Just as we need food daily,
including bread, so we need spiritual food daily.
Have you been growing spiritually? Are you
getting a proper spiritual diet of prayer, Bible
lessons, and fellowship?

DAY 2

SHOWBREAD

EXODUS 25:30 *Put the bread of the presence on this table to be before me at all times.*

 Activity

Read about shewbread in *Leviticus 24:5-9* and *Exodus 25:23-30*. Place one piece of bread on the bread plate for each person in the family.

 Talk about it

God told Moses to keep the bread of presence on the altar at all times. This bread, called the "shewbread" or "showbread", was consecrated and only the Levites were allowed to eat it. The twelve loaves of bread, one for each tribe, placed on the table in the Holy Place, symbolized God's care for His people.

The term 'showbread' means the bread of presence. It reminds us to use bread as a reminder of Jesus, the Bread of Life, and to show others to Jesus. Our table is Holy because Jesus is with us. We should approach our meals knowing that Jesus hears what we say and how we treat one another. Remember each tribe, represented by a loaf, was significant to God. Our plate contains one piece of bread for each family member as a reminder that each of us is important to God.

 Further exploration

Only the priests could eat the bread. Read about the choice of priests in *Numbers 17:1-13*. Then read what God says in *1 Peter 2:9*.

 Do

Enjoy the bread and remember God wants you to be a leader – a spiritual leader!

DAY 3

SERVING THE WORD!

MATTHEW 4:4 *Jesus answered, "It is written: 'Man does not live on bread alone, but on every word that comes from the mouth of God.' "*

 Activity

Write down everyone's favorite Bible verse or Bible story. Put them on the bread plate. At meal time, take one of the Bible verses and serve up a favorite word from God!!

 Talk about it

Discuss spiritual food and our need for God's Word! We need to digest God's Word by understanding it and taking it in to our hearts by memorizing it and living it.

Action in Following Jesus

.Happy the family that knows little surprises bring blessings for they have hope!

These activities look at a small man to illustrate that size does not matter.

— MATERIALS —

✧ small ladder or step stool
✧ Biblical costumes or towels and ties for making Biblical headdresses

DAY 1

PREPARING FOR DRAMA

LUKE 19:4 *So he ran ahead and climbed a sycamore-fig tree to see him, since Jesus was coming that way,*

 Activity

Read about Zacchaeus in Luke 19:1-10. Prepare to dramatize it. Assign parts in the script with the smallest person for Zacchaeus. Let the tallest person be the tree, or use a small ladder or chair for the tree. Let each person stand on the ladder and look at the others from that perspective. Make simple costumes.

 Talk about it

Jesus knows everyone's name and what they do and think. He found Zacchaeus. How prepared are you to be with Jesus right now? Zacchaeus was small but he saw above the crowds. Do we work at seeing Jesus through a crowded life?

DAY 2

ACTION

Act out the account of Jesus meeting Zacchaeus by using the script.

LUKE 19:10 *For the Son of Man came to seek and save what was lost.*

DAY 3

FINALE

1 PETER 3:8 *Finally all of you, live in harmony with one another, be sympathetic, love as brothers, be compassionate and humble.*

 Activity

Each person sits on the floor while others stand and talk.

 Talk about it

How do you think Zacchaeus felt when Jesus spoke? Why did he decide to repay people he cheated? How would you feel if Jesus came today? How did Zacchaeus respond when people called him a sinner? Do we worry about what people will say if we tell them we are Christians? Do we help others see Jesus?

Narrator
Zacchaeus was a little man
Who learned in life to say, I can.
Too short to see the Lord who was surrounded by a clan,
Zacchaeus thought of a good plan.

Zacchaeus
If I climb high up in this tree
Then Jesus I will surely see.
I've got to know if what I heard is true.
Oh, all the things they say this man can do!
Here He comes right to this tree,
And now He's looking up at me!!!

Jesus
Zacchaeus, hurry and come down,
For today I must stay at your home in town!

Crowd
Oh no! Oh no! Oh no no no!
That man is full of sin!
Eat with Him and our hearts you cannot win!!

Zacchaeus
Lord, you are a wonder to behold!
Now I believe all that I was told.
You know my name and where to find me!
I am thankful that my home is where you want to be.

Crowd
Oh no! Oh no! Oh no no no!
That man is full of sin!
Eat with Him and our hearts you cannot win!!

Zacchaeus
Oh, Lord what they say is true!
But listen to what I'm gonna do.
Anyone I ever cheated I will repay times four
And half of all I own I will give to the poor!

Jesus
Zacchaeus, you are a son of Abraham, a kin to me!
And this day all in your house are set free!
The Son has come to seek and find the lost.
The Son of Man will save them – He'll pay the cost.

Narrator
Jesus wants to come to your house, too.
He wants to share bread with each of you.
No matter your size He knows your name.
He loves you and for you He came.
From your sins He will set you free.
And you don't even have to climb a tree!

Processing TV Viewing

Happy is the family that tunes in to their children's activities for they will be united.

Parents need to observe their children's habits including their TV viewing habits. This week take time to watch TV together and learn to process shows, using these shows as a springboard for teaching.

> ### — MATERIALS —
>
> ✧ *TV*
> ✧ *popcorn with no seasoning*
> ✧ *popcorn with various seasonings/ flavorings (cheese, salt, butter)*
> ✧ *Bible and concordance*

DAY 1

OBSERVATIONS

HEBREWS 13:17 *Obey your leaders and submit to their authority. They keep watch over you as men who must give an account.*

 Activity

Watch a TV show as a family. Then use one of these forms as a guideline for processing the show.

 Talk about it

Respond to the questionnaire, then discuss the show and the thoughts asked about on the form. Also discuss:

How would Jesus respond to the same situation?

How did the show view children, old people, women, and men?

Who liked the show and why?

Do children need permission to watch TV shows? Who should decide which shows are okay to be watched?

Analyzing the TV Viewing

1. Name of show.

2. Brief description of the episode.

3. Message of show.

4. Values talked about or taught.

5. Main characters.

6. Any characters you identified with (have felt like that person or would like to be like).

7. Identify some clothing and items on show.

8. Rate expense of the above items: cheap, expensive, affordable.

9. Was any humor making fun of someone? If yes, who and why?

10. Problem presented in show.

11. Was problem solved? How or why?

12. Was there any violence? How much and why?

13. Was there any bad language used? If yes, did it need to be used?

14. Would Jesus enjoy this show? Why or why not?

15. Should this show be watched again?

16. What commercials were shown during the show time?

17. What were the messages of the commercials?

TV and younger children

1. What was the name of the show?

2. What were the names of the people or animals on the show?

3. What happened?

4. Can you draw a picture of your favorite part?

5. What did you like about the show?

6. Was anything sad, scary, or bad on the show?

7. Was anything funny? Did anyone do or say something that made you laugh?

8. What part would you like to play on the show? Why? Draw a picture of you in the show.

9. Did anyone get hurt?

10. Would Jesus like this show? Why or why not?

11. Did they have to fix a problem? How did they fix it?

12. What commercials did you watch?

DAY 2

PROCESSING THE SHOW

PSALM 119:66 *Teach me knowledge and good judgment, for I believe in your commands.*

Preparation

As parents take time before the study to look up Bible verses in a concordance that deal with the message of the show watched on day one.

Activity and discussion

1. Serve popcorn some with no seasonings or flavorings and some seasoned. Talk about how flat one tastes in comparison to the seasoned food.

2. Read in The Living Bible – *Matthew 5:13* "You are the world's seasoning to make it tolerable. If you lose your flavor, what will happen to the world? And you yourselves will be thrown out and trampled underfoot as worthless." Also read *Colossians 4:6* that speaks of our speech being the seasoning, as salt, so that we may know how to respond to each person.

3. Who should season our lives? Other people may provide food for thought but we need godly seasoning, the right flavor of Christ, in our lives.

4. Read Bible verses relating to the message of the TV show viewed on day one. How did it measure up to God's standard?

DAY 3

SET GROUND RULES FOR TV VIEWING

PHILIPPIANS 4:8 *Finally, brothers, whatever is true, whatever is noble, whatever is right, whatever is pure, whatever is lovely, whatever is admirable- if anything is excellent or praiseworthy- think about such things.*

Activity

Set ground rules for TV viewing. Talk about how many hours per day or week; types of shows; alternate activities; priority of TV, chores, and schoolwork, etc. Try a minute of reading (the Bible) for each minute of watching TV!

Talk about it

Do the rules you set make sense. How much TV viewing is done? When? What type of shows? What else do family members do in free time to relax?

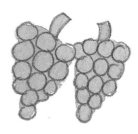

Agape Meal

Happy is the family that knows the body needs more than food for they will be well-nourished!

Children are taught about nutrition and how important it is to eat good food. These activities teach them about the importance of the right spiritual food!

— MATERIALS —

❖ *paper and pencil*
❖ *scissors*
❖ *bread*
❖ *grapes or grape juice*
❖ *plates*

DAY 1

INVITATION

LUKE 24:35 *Then the two told what had happened on the way, and how Jesus was recognized by them when he broke the bread.*

 Preparation

Copy, cut, and fold the "bunch of grapes" invitation below. Add the date and time for this week's Agape Meal. Every family member should receive an invitation.

 Activity

Read the invitation. Read *Luke 24:13-35* of the walk to Emmaus or read about the Lord's Supper in *Luke 22:14-23*.

 Talk about it

Agape means both love and charity. What did Jesus mean when He said, "I am the Bread of Life"? Make plans about what to wear and what music to play.

16

DAY 2

AGAPE MEAL

ACTS 2:42 *They devoted themselves to the apostle's teaching and to the fellowship, to the breaking of bread and to prayer.*

 Preparation

Let children cut paper loaves of bread, with the top of the loaves on folded paper. Inside, write a Bible verse. On the covers, write people's names.

Set a loaf of bread on a bread plate surrounded with grapes. Serve with juice.

 Activity

Read *Luke 24: 30-31*. Then, break off pieces of bread. Pass out grapes, reminding them how Jesus shared bread and the fruit of the grapevine, at the Last Supper. Let everyone read and comment on their verses.

DAY 3

SPIRITUAL FOODS

JOHN 6:35 *Then Jesus declared, "I am the bread of life. He who comes to me will never go hungry, and he who believes in me will never be thirsty."*

 Activity

Give each person a paper heart or draw hearts in journals. Inside the heart, let everyone write or draw a memory of when they felt loved.

 Talk about it

Discuss the Agape meal. Bread fills us up for a little while, but love keeps us full, especially God's love. The first Christians celebrated together with love feasts or agape meals. Jesus offers us an unending supply of love – a feast of love which will keep our hearts filled! Take time to talk about communion at church.

Prayer

*Happy is the family that knows the importance
of prayer for they will abide in God.*

Use these activities to teach some basics of prayer, a great tool for life!

— MATERIALS —

✧ *paper*
✧ *white cardboard*
✧ *markers including a red one*
✧ *scissors*
✧ *glue or tape*
✧ *small piece of red felt (optional)*

DAY 1

ACTS BOOKMARK

The acronym "ACTS" contains prayer guidelines.

DEUTERONOMY 6:4 *Hear, O Israel! The Lord is our God, the Lord is one.*

 Activity

Follow the pattern below left to make a heart bookmark. Decorate it. Color the heart red or glue on a red felt heart as a reminder that God wants His love felt.

 Talk about the shape

The heart at the top and the shape of a one (1) for the rest of the bookmark. The one (1) remind us the Lord comes first and there is only one God!

Adoration
Confession
Thanksgiving
Supplication

DAY 2

PRAYER TAKES ACTION

PSALM 99:5 *Exalt the Lord our God, and worship at his footstool; he is Holy.*

The **A** represents adoration which means to give praise or applause to God.

 Talk about it

Words of praise for God.

1 JOHN 1:9 *If we confess our sins, he is faithful and just and will forgive us our sins and purify us from all unrighteousness.*

The **C** is for 'contrition' or 'confessing'. We confess and God forgives. The **C** also reminds us of the word 'change'. God forgives us and helps us change.

 Talk about it

Who does sin hurt? Talk about forgiveness.

DAY 3

THANKS AND REQUESTS!

1 THESSALONIANS 5:18 *Give thanks in all circumstances, for this is God's will for you in Christ Jesus.*

The **T** is for 'Thanksgiving'. Thank God for His provisions. Thanking God puts the focus on God as our provider rather than on ourselves.

 Activity

Let everyone thank God for one thing!

1 JOHN 5:14-15 *This is the confidence we have in approaching God: that if we ask anything according to his will, he hears us. And if we know that he hears us – whatever we ask – we know that we have what we asked of him.*

S is for 'Supplication'. It comes from the word supply. Supplication means to ask. This is the last letter because we should think of ourselves last and put God first.

Vision

Happy is the family that knows that sight needs insight for they will have faith!

These activities help open eyes and minds in understanding.

> — MATERIALS —
>
> ✦ paper and pencils
> ✦ scissors
> ✦ book with some optical illusions in it (optional)
> ✦ tray
> ✦ objects relating to Bible stories
>   (NOTE: just use the ones available such as grapes, fish crackers, a container with a little oil, wash cloth or towel, a feather, a broken roll, plastic pairs of animals and a toy boat, toy lion with a toy man)

DAY 1

EYE SPY

JOHN 20:29 *Then Jesus told him, "Because you have seen me, you have believed; blessed are those who have not seen and yet have believed."*

Activity

Cut out a paper eye and use it playing this game!

Everyone leaves the room except one person. This one person hides the eye in plain sight, with at least a portion showing. Everyone re-enters and without touching anything, searches for the eye. Upon finding the eye, he or she sits down without revealing the location. The last person to spy the eye picks it up and hides it next.

Talk about it

Some people take longer to spy the eye than other people. Just as the eye was nearby, in plain sight, so Jesus is near to everyone. Yet there are people who seem blind, unable to see Jesus or unable to believe. Does it ever seem that Jesus is not listening? Well, God is right there with us, but maybe you are looking in the wrong place for Him and for your answered prayers!

DAY 2

BIBLE ON-TRAYS

MARK 8:18 *Do you have eyes but fail to see, and ears but fail to hear? And don't you remember?*

 Activity

Place items on the tray that relate to Bible stories and see how many Bible events each person can name from seeing the objects.

○ grapes for the wedding in Cana *(John 2:1-11)*

○ fish crackers for the feeding of the 5000
(Matthew 14:13-21)

○ a container with a little oil for Elisha and the widow *(2 Kings 4:1-7)*

○ wash cloth or towel for Jesus washing disciples' feet *(John 13:5)*

○ a feather for the bird providing bread for Elijah *(1 Kings 17:6)*

○ a broken roll for Jesus breaking bread at Emmaus *(Luke 24:18)*

○ animals and toy boat for Noah and the ark
(Genesis 7:1-4)

○ lion for Daniel in the lion's den
(Daniel 6:16-23)

 Note

For younger children use items that relate to one Bible event, such as a boat, rainbow sticker, and animals for Noah and the ark. Guess the Bible story.

 Talk about it

Imagery helps us remember. Jesus used familiar images in telling parables. Some people could not understand the messages and lessons in the parables. People had to think about what was said to find the spiritual truths. Jesus wants us to dig and search for truth and meaning.

DAY 3

OPTICAL ILLUSIONS AND SIGHT

2 CORINTHIANS 5:7 *We live by faith, not by sight.*

 Activity

Look at a book of optical illusions. Here are 2 optical illusions to try:

1. Hold your pointer fingers in front of your face. Bring the 2 fingers about 1 inch apart and about 2 inches in front of your eyes. Stare at the space between your fingers. Do you see a piece of your finger floating in the air?

2. Place an empty toilet paper roll over your eye and look through it. Keep both eyes open. Hold your other hand open against the side of the roll about midway along the roll. It appears that there is a hole in your hand!

 Talk about it

Our eyes can be tricked. We need to follow God in faith and not look at the world or at other people.

Song and Worship

Happy is the family that knows music lightens the heart for they will praise God!

Music and songs fill our world from the TV and radio to the church. Take time as parents to share music through singing and listening to songs.

— MATERIALS —

✧ words or tapes of favorite songs (and tape player for tapes)
✧ a bunch of pennies
✧ an empty box

DAY 1

SHARING FAVORITE SONGS

EXODUS 15:2 *The Lord is my strength and my song; he has become my salvation. He is my God, and I will praise him, my father's God and I will exalt him.*

Activity and discussion

1. Let each person name his or her favorite song. Listen to these favorites. What songs does each person of the family enjoy? Are they Christian songs or a different type? What is the message in the song and what do the words mean? Is it a funny song, a sad song, or a happy one?

2. What song did your parents choose for their wedding song? Why? Can they share any story behind their choice? Special celebrations in the Bible also had special songs. Read *Luke 2:13-14* where the angels sang. What were they celebrating?

3. Listen to some school songs. What is the message? Is it a fighting song or one of unity? Do your parents have school songs they still remember? Does each student in the family have a school song? If you are home-schooled, can you write your own school song?

4. Listen to today's verse again. What does it mean to say, "The Lord is my song"?

DAY 2

SINGING IN THE BIBLE

ACTS 16:25 *About midnight Paul and Silas were praying and singing hymns to God, and the other prisoners were listening to them.*

 Activity and discussion

Look up singing and music in the Bible.

1. God's people won battles with music. Read about one such battle in Joshua chapter 6.

TRY IT: *Music produces vibrations. Put a stack of pennies on an empty box and tap the box. Watch the pennies vibrate and fall down.*

2. In 2 *Kings 3:14-16*, a musician delivered God's message on how He would provide water for them. Have you ever gotten a message from Christian music?

3. After the Last Supper, Jesus sang a hymn with His disciples, according to *Matthew 26:30*. We do not know the name of the hymn but we do know that Jesus felt the need to sing as he approached the upcoming crucifixion.

TRY IT: *Sing a hymn together. The next time you are sad or hurting, sing hymns.*

Paul and Silas sang in jail. Read about it in *Acts 16:25-34*. The singing led to the baptism of the jailer and his household. There was an earthquake that scared the jailer but not the singers.

TRY IT: *Next time you are in a storm, try singing!*

DAY 3

SINGSPIRATION

PSALM 33:1 *Sing joyfully to the Lord, you righteous; it is fitting for the upright to praise him.*

 Activity

Read these verses in the Bible which are reminders to sing:

1. *Ephesians 5:19-20* tell us to have a melody to God in our hearts.

2. *Colossians 3:16* tells us to teach others about God in songs.

3. In *James 5:13* we are told that if we are happy we should sing!

Have a sing-a-long or listen to Christian music

 Talk about it

Singing can help us to praise God and make us feel joyful. After singing and listening, talk about how it made you feel about God.

Creative Storytelling

Happy is the family that shares stories
for they will build memories!

Jesus told parables or stories to teach. Families can illustrate these stories with a story wall and learn to share personal stories.

— MATERIALS —

❖ felt, large enough to partially cover a wall in playroom or bedroom (4 feet high or large enough to cover a table)
❖ felt scraps
❖ staple gun and staples, or thumb tacks
❖ fabric scissors
❖ fusible webbing (optional)

DAY 1

STORY WALL

MATTHEW 13:34 *Jesus spoke all these things to the crowd in parables, he did not say anything to them without using a parable.*

 Activity

Create a wall or area covered with felt.

1. Iron under the raw edges of the felt.

2. If desired, hem with fusible webbing.

3. Staple or tack the felt to the wall.

Or, if not feasible for a wall, cover a table or box top with the felt.

4. Cut out felt into shapes – various sizes of circles, squares, rectangles and triangle can be used to make people, boats, mountains, and other items in the stories. Use cookie cutters and coloring book pictures, if desired, as patterns for more elaborate felt cutouts.

 Talk about it

Jesus taught people with stories. Why did Jesus use stories to teach? Look up the answer Jesus gave in *Matthew 13:11-13*.

Decorate the wall (or table cloth) with the cutouts. Use them to help tell the stories Jesus told. As pieces are cut out and stuck on the felt, talk about how the thoughts stuck in people's minds better when told in a story.

DAY 2

A FISHY TALE

MATTHEW 17:27 *But so that we may not offend them, go to the lake and throw out your line. Take the first fish you catch; open its mouth and you will find a four-drachma coin. Take it and give it to them for my tax and yours.*

 Read

Read in *Matthew 17:24-27*, about the time tax collectors asked Peter if Jesus paid taxes and how a fish provided the tax money.

 Activity

Use a felt circle and triangle to make a fish. Use a smaller circle placed under the fish for the coin used to pay the taxes. Make people with upright triangular shapes and circles for heads.

Now tell the event for today's verse on the story wall.

 Talk about it

How could Jesus be certain that the first fish caught would have the right coin in its mouth? Let the children take turns retelling this event.

DAY 3

OUR STORY!

2 CORINTHIANS 3:3 *You show that you are a letter from Christ, the result of our ministry, written not with ink but with the Spirit of the living God, not on tablets of stone but on tablets of human hearts.*

 Activity

Use the felt cutouts and story wall to let each person tell about their day or an event in their life.

 Talk about it

It is through daily actions in life that others see who follows Christ. Talk about the day's events on the story wall and how Jesus can be seen in daily life. Children's actions also reflect the lessons taught them by parents and others. What do others see in you? What is in your heart?

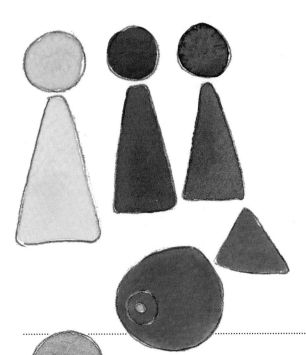

Consequences

Happy is the family who knows actions produce consequences for they will learn responsibility.

Science teaches that every action causes an equal and opposite reaction. These activities teach responsibility for reactions caused by actions.

— MATERIALS —

✧ 2 clear glasses
✧ food coloring (red or blue)
✧ Optional: Someone wearing roller blades
✧ basket of apples

DAY 1

ACTIONS CAUSE REACTIONS

LUKE 6:38 *Give and it will be given to you. A good measure, pressed down, shaken together. and running over, will be poured into your lap. For with the measure you use, it will be measured to you.*

 Activity

1. On a sidewalk or a paved driveway mark a starting line and a finish line.

2. Have the person wearing roller blades hold the basket of apples and stand at the starting line with his or her back to the finish line.

3. One at a time, let the skaters throw the apples forward to someone a few feet behind the starting line. This action will result in the skater moving backward toward the finish line.

4. Continue this until the skater reaches the finish line or runs out of apples.

 What happens

Each time an apple is tossed a reaction occurs. Throwing the apple causes the roller blades to move the opposite way, moving the skaters closer to the finish line!

 Talk about it

In science, every action causes an equal and opposite reaction. We read that when we give, it will be given to us by the same measure – equal but opposite. What happens when you cause pain by unkind words or actions? And what happens when you cause joy by giving love and smiles?

DAY 2

SENDING AND RECEIVING

ECCLESIASTES 11:1 *Cast your bread upon the waters, for after many days you will find it again*

 Activity

Throw an apple (or ball) straight up in the air several times.

 Talk about it

The apple returns. What happens when you throw it harder?

To cast bread takes much more work than casting a fishing line. Why? First the bread has to be made. Secondly, to throw bread on the water seems to have no purpose. When we take a spiritual risk, we trust in God for the results. What do you want to do in the future? Will this just happen? Will it take work and trust?

 Notes

Bible scholars have questioned the meaning of this verse. One explanation is that it meant sending out ships that took about three years to return with merchandise and trusting that the voyage would be completed.

Others think it meant that seed cast at the river's edge might be upset by flooding, but the flooding causes topsoil to be replenished and the seed would sprout down river and be bountiful in unexpected places.

 Deeper questions

The bread cast is the fruit of our labor. What if that fruit is rotten? What if we cast out lies and our bad actions? Will that come back to us also after many days? What if we cast love by serving others? Think of something to do this week that could have a positive reaction and then plan to do it.

DAY 3

CONSEQUENCES THAT SPREAD

JAMES 3:5 *Likewise the tongue is a small part of the body, but it makes great boasts. Consider what a great forest is set on fire by a small spark.*

 Activity

Take 2 glasses of water and add a drop of red or blue food coloring to each. Stir or gently shake the water in one glass. Watch what happens. How long does it take to spread the color. Can you take out the color?

 Talk about it

How do rumors spread? Do we ever use our mouths to spread evil? What else can be spread using our mouths? Do you ever gossip? Lie? Once a rumor has been spread, like the yeast in the dough, can it be easily removed?

 **Apply**

Decide on one way to spread good news with your tongue!

Communication

Happy is the family that openly communicates for they will have open hearts!

Communication is needed for a close knit family. Parents can help children learn to communicate with these activities.

— MATERIALS —

❖ *empty jar*
❖ *paper*
❖ *pencils*
❖ *index cards*

DAY 1

OPEN JARS

JOHN 2: 7 *Jesus said to the servants, "Fill the jars with water," so they filled them to the brim.*

 Activity

Start an open jar policy. Sometimes children want to ask questions but don't want to reveal their identity or ask in front of others. Sometimes people have a burning question, but no one has time to answer and later it is forgotten.

Have an open jar or container where questions can be placed. From time to time, take out one or all the questions and answer or discuss them as a family.

 Talk about it

The water jars at the wedding in Cana were open and ready to have their contents changed into wine. We too are vessels who need open minds that are ready to change. Be ready to let God work on the inside, changing your minds and hearts.

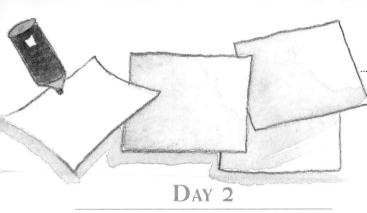

DAY 2

LISTENING AND RESPONDING WITH OPENNESS

MATTHEW 11:15 *He who has ears, let him hear.*

 Activity

Give an index card and pencil to everyone. Let each person write down something that bothers them or a problem they are facing. Turn over the cards. Now shuffle them and pass them out, blank side up. Have everyone write down a nice thought without looking at what was written. Now let each person read both sides of the card in their hand.

 Talk about it

How does listening help? To blankly pass out advice does not help or encourage people. Now read each problem and discuss possible solutions!

DAY 3

GROUND RULES FOR OPEN DISCUSSIONS

COLOSSIANS 3:15 *Let the peace of Christ rule in your hearts, since as members of one body you were called to peace. And be thankful.*

 Activity and discussion

We are called to peace and unity. This does not mean we always agree, but in peace and love we can listen and make group decisions.

Read Acts 15 to discover how early church leaders solved a dispute with open discussion. Note how scripture verses played a part in their dialogue. Set ground rules for honest discussions that encourage input from all members, as well as listening to God's input. A family forum does not mean that parents reliquish authority, but it simply means that parents open their hearts to new ideas.

Here are some suggestions:

1. Let everyone have time to talk. Don't correct or challenge.

2. Keep what is discussed at family devotions in the family.

3. Allow time for answers. Silence gives time for people to think before speaking.

4. Be polite and considerate – don't interrupt a speaker.

5. Be active listeners – listen to what other people say. You may need to ask questions or repeat what the other person said to see if you fully understood.

6. Accept opinions – this does not mean that you agree.

7. Avoid lectures. Children should avoid simply filing a list of complaints and accusations.

8. Have a comfortable setting – informal and relaxed.

9. Use eye contact – look at the person speaking.

10. Read and let everyone respond to related Bible verses. Note that God's values and biblical standards are to be held up as the standard for living.

11. Remember that love is the guiding light from God.

 Talk about it

Colossians 3:15 is a reminder to let love unite us and the peace of Christ rule. Discuss the guidelines. Will they work in your family or do they need to be modified? How many do you already do? Which ones need to be worked on?

Fishing for Success

Happy is the family that knows success cannot be measured for they will accomplish much!

Jesus told His disciples the time had come for a career change. In reflecting on the apostle's fishing adventure we can learn about success.

— MATERIALS —

✧ colored paper
✧ paper clips
✧ string
✧ short sticks or chopsticks
✧ magnetic strips (or magnets)
✧ scissors

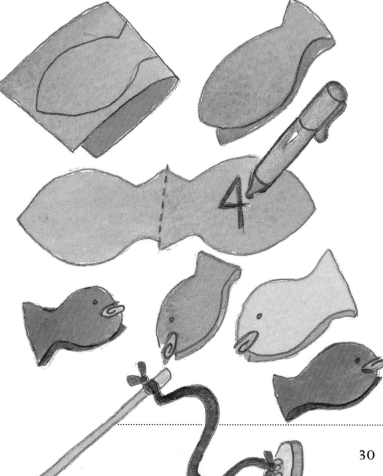

DAY 1

WHAT A CATCH!

LUKE 5:4 *When he had finished speaking, he said to Simon, "Put out into deep water, and let down the nets for a catch."*

 Preparation

Make a fishing game.

1. Fold colored paper in half.

2. Draw fish with the fold as the end of the tail fins of the fish.

3. Cut out the fish but do not cut the fold.

4. Then open up the fish. Write one number, between 0 and 10, on the inside of each fish.

5. Close each fish with a paper clip for the mouth. Make lots of fish!

Then make fishing poles.

1. Tie a 12 inch piece of string onto the end of a stick.

2. On the other end of the string attach a magnet.

 Activity

Read about Peter's big catch in *Luke 5: 4-10.* Put the fish inside a bowl. Now go fishing until all the fish are caught. If it's too hard to catch the fish, dump them out on the floor. Keep everyone's catch separate but don't open up the fish today!

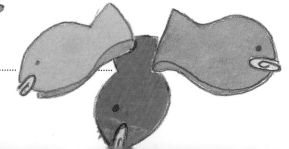

Talk about it

It's easy and fun to catch these paper fish. When the fish can be seen it is even easier. What helped the disciples? When we are failing at something, what should we do? Have you ever been amazed at the results of prayer?

DAY 2

FISHING GAME

MATTHEW 4:19 *"Come follow me," Jesus said, "and I will make you fishers of men."*

 Activity

Let each person open up the fish they caught and add up the numbers. The one with the highest total wins!

 Talk about it

Talk about what it means to be a fisher of men, to help others believe in God. Each fish caught represents a person. The numbers inside represent how many persons (fish) were caught. A disciple may catch someone who becomes a great church leader! A zero represents those people a disciple thinks he caught but who never really believed. God knows if the fish (person) caught became a great fisherman.

God does not measure success by outward appearance such as a large stack of fish, but by what's inside the heart!

DAY 3

FISHING FOR SUCCESS!

JOHN 21:13 *Jesus came, took the bread, and gave it to them, and did the same with the fish.*

 Preparation

Cut out paper fish. Write a Bible verse about success on each fish, such as *Matthew 6:32-34; Joshua 1:7-9; Acts 20:32; Psalm 119:105;* and *John 15:7.*

 Activity

Let everyone take one fish. Look up the verses and read them.

 Talk about it

God's view of success. The right equipment helps in fishing. A fisherman uses a good line, or net of well woven line. The lines we use as fishers of men are Bible verses! If a person read and learned one verse each week, how many would be learned in one year? Start by learning today's verse.

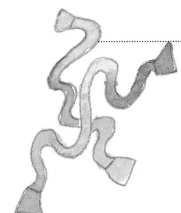

Prayer Hindrances

Happy is the family that removes obstacles
for their prayers will be heard!

Have fun with ropes and obstacle courses while learning about prayer!

— MATERIALS —

✧ rope for tug of war
✧ obstacles and objects to climb over and under for an obstacle course

---

DAY 1

YIELDING TO GOD OR TUG OF WARS!

1 PETER 5:7 *Cast all your anxiety on him because he cares for you.*

 Activity

Hold a family tug of war. Try these activities:

1. Try balancing the weight and strength on each side.

2. Try having the head of the family on one side and everyone else on the other side.

3. Tie a rope to a door knob on the side without the hinge. Have one person stand on the inside with the door closed. Let other family members pull on the rope and yell for help. Let the person on the inside try to open the door to come help. What happens?

 Talk about it

When we give our cares to God do we try to tell Him what to do or do we try to take them back? Do we continue to worry after we give a problem to God? Do we sometimes ask God for help but don't let Him in to help? Isn't this like pulling a door closed while asking for someone to come in and help?

 Apply

Think of one problem now and give it to God, believing that he hears you and that he will take care of it. Write the problem down in a prayer journal and in a few weeks write down your feelings. Note whether you have received the answer yet!

DAY 2

OBSTACLE COURSES

PSALM 66:18 *If I had cherished sin in my heart, the Lord would not have listened.*

 Activity

Set up a path. Put chairs, toys, or other objects in the way of the path. Now have people try to run in a straight line along the path. Blindfold one person at a time and try to verbally guide them around the objects. Spin the person around a few times then hold their hand and guide them around the obstacles. For the last person blindfolded, quietly remove the obstacles and tell them to walk along the path.

 Talk about it

Is it easy to go straight with a large obstacle in the way? Can we get to the other end of the path quickly? Sin can be an obstacle that keeps us from God and keeps our prayers from getting to God. We may be blinded to our sins, unwilling to confess them, unwilling to let Jesus remove them. God wants to guide us and direct our path but we cannot clutter the path with sins!!

 Pray

Ask for forgiveness to any unconfessed sin.

DAY 3

PRAYING WITHOUT HINDRANCES

MATTHEW 21:22 *If you believe, you will receive whatever you ask for in prayer.*

JAMES 4:3 *When you ask, you do not receive, because you ask with wrong motives, that you may spend what you get on your pleasures.*

 Activity

Think of one answer you received in prayer.

 Talk about it

Talk about the answered prayer. Did you believe God could answer it and that he would? Why did you pray for that? Was it a good reason?

Now talk about something you want to pray for at this time. Why do you ask for this? Are there any hindrances to prayer in your life? Are you willing to let God answer it however He chooses? Do you have any sin to confess?

 Do

List each person's most important prayer request. Pray together for all the prayers. Then post the list on the refrigerator. Check off the prayers as answers come.

Flower Puppets

Happy is the family that rejoices as their children blossom for they will have the fragrance of Christ!

Puppetry provides opportunities for children to express their faith.

— MATERIALS —

✦ sheets of paper 8.5 x 11 inches (21.5 x 28cm)
✦ crayons and markers
✦ colored paper
✦ scissors
✦ glue

DAY 1

MAKE THE PUPPETS

MATTHEW 6:28-29 *And why do you worry about clothes? See how the lilies of the field grow. They do not labor or spin. Yet I tell you that not even Solomon in all his splendor was dressed like one of these.*

Activity

1. Fold a sheet of paper lengthwise in thirds, with both sides folded into the center. Glue or tape the edge of the top fold down. This forms a rectangle.

2. Mark 6.5 inches (25cm) from rectangle's bottom edge. Fold along this line. One end will be longer than the other.

3. Fold the longer end in half so open edge meets fold. Turn over paper and fold shorter side in half the same way. This forms a puppet with a protruding bottom chin and two openings- one for the thumb and one for fingers. Moving the thumb up and down works the puppet.

4. Make the flower: Cut a flower from paper, at least 3 inches (9 cm) wide.

5. Cut across flower a little below the center. Glue top of flower to top of puppet and bottom of flower to bottom of puppet.

6. Draw eyes and upper lip on top part. Draw lower lip on bottom part.

7. Open puppet's mouth. Draw lines connecting the lips.

8. Color flower and mouth.

9. Add a stem to back bottom of puppet.

Talk about it

Look at how a piece of paper was changed into a puppet. God changes us, too. What did Jesus tells us to learn from flowers?

DAY 2

CREATE THE MESSAGE

ROMANS 1:20 *For since the creation of the world God's invisible qualities — his eternal power and divine nature — have been clearly seen, being understood from what has been made, so that men are without excuse.*

 Activity

Make up rhymes for the flowers. Here are a few examples:

DAISY	This daisy does not play
	He loves me, He loves me not
	For all the days of my life
	I know God loves me
	He loves me a lot!
TULIP	I'm a tulip with 2 lips
	That open and close
	I tell others
	Jesus died and rose!

 Talk about it

The puppet looks pretty, but to be useful a script and actions are needed. We too, need to open up to be useful. God's creations provide messages. Let each person talk about one creation God made that amazes them.

DAY 3

BLOSSOMING WITH JOY

MATTHEW 25:21 *His master replied, "Well done, good and faithful servant! You have been faithful with a few things; I will put you in charge of many things. Come and share your master's happiness!"*

 Activity

Perform your puppet show, with the flowers reciting their rhymes.

Talk about it

Read *Matthew 25:14-30* This is called the parable of the talents. One talent is possibly worth one thousand dollars. We also use the word talent to talk about our abilities. God wants us to use what He gives us whether it is money or abilities. The puppets won't help other people if they sit on a shelf. Think of ways to help other people. Choose one of the ideas and use the puppets in telling the story

Bread Making

Happy is the family that knows it takes more than people to make a family for they will be caring.

In making bread, ingredients need to be mixed. These activities help children learn what makes a happy family.

> — MATERIALS —
>
> ✧ favorite bread recipe
> ✧ ingredients to make the bread
> ✧ baking pan
> ✧ mixing bowl and spoon
> ✧ bread and sandwich fillings
>
> (NOTE: If this is a busy week, buy a package mix for bread)

DAY 1

BREAD THAT'S NOT BREAD

JAMES 1:22 *Do not merely listen to the word, and so deceive yourselves. Do what it says.*

 Activity

Tell everyone that you're going to share a very special bread with them. Show them the recipe and ingredients and ask them to pass around the bread and eat some of it. If someone objects that it is not bread yet, remind them that it is a very good recipe, tested and that everything for the bread is already here. Then ask what the problem seems to be.

 Talk about it

What might happen if we never mixed the bread ingredients together or baked it? Flour and other ingredients eaten separately would not taste very good nor satisfy our hunger. How did it feel to be asked to eat the unbaked ingredients?

Some people say they are Christians but seldom live as Christians. They have the recipe – the Bible. They know verses. Maybe they were baptized and go to church. Do we need to have Jesus mixed into our daily life? What can we do now to live according to God's Word? Can a family be a family just by placing people under the same roof? What is it that makes people a family and what is it that makes a house a home?

Family Devotional Builder

DAY 2

MAKE THE BREAD

ROMANS 12:2 *Do not conform any longer to the pattern of this world, but be transformed by the renewing of your mind. Then you will be able to test and approve what God's will is- his good, pleasing and perfect will.*

 Activity

Following the recipe, make the bread. Talk about how to test or know when the bread is done. Enjoy eating the bread after it cools.

 Talk about it

Does the bread look and taste better after mixing and cooking the ingredients? Are we better when we read and follow God's Word? The oven transformed the mixed ingredients into bread. The warmth of God's love transforms us. Talk about how God has changed each of us.

DAY 3

SANDWICHES FROM BREAD (*FILLED WITH THE HOLY SPIRIT*)

ACTS 2:4 *And all of them were filled with the Holy Spirit and began to speak in with other tongues, as the Spirit enabled them.*

 Activity

Make various sandwiches, with all sorts of fillings – fruit jellies, meats, tuna, etc. Cut the sandwiches into quarters so each person can try a different type. Enjoy eating the sandwiches. While enjoying the sandwiches, read *Acts 2:1-4*.

 Talk about it

Talk about how the fillings changed the taste of the bread. How does the Holy Spirit fill our lives and helps us be closer to Jesus? One bread but the results were different because of the different fillings. There are many gifts and fruits of the Holy Spirit. We are each unique and God has different plans for each person.

 Look up

Look up the gifts of the Spirit in *Romans 12:3-8* and *1 Corinthians 12: 28*.

Look up the fruit of the Spirit in *Galatians 5:22*.

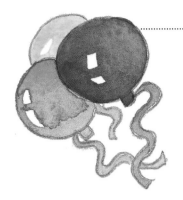

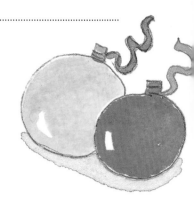

WEEK SEVENTEEN

Power

*Happy is the family that knows the source
of power for they will be energized!*

These activities on power help children understand the Holy Spirit's power.

--- MATERIALS ---

✧ *2 soda bottles*
✧ *bag of balloons*
✧ *string*
✧ *straws*
✧ *clear tape*
✧ *2 pkg. yeast*
✧ *warm water*
✧ *½ cup whole wheat flour*
✧ *½ cup grape juice*
✧ *2 bowls*
✧ *funnel*
✧ *spoon*

DAY 1

BALLOONS WITH NO POWER

2 CORINTHIANS 12:9 *But he said to me, "My grace is sufficient for you, my power is made perfect in weakness." Therefore I will boast all the more gladly about my weakness, so that Christ's power may rest on me.*

 Activity

Try to throw the uninflated balloons up in the air and catch them. Try bouncing them. Blow up the balloons. Tie them off. Throw them up and catch them. Bounce them.

 Talk about it

The balloons are lighter and easier to play with when they have air inside. The air expands the balloon. Without God's love we are flat. We need to be filled with God's love. Then we will feel lighter and able to bounce back from problems.

DAY 2

EXPERIMENT — YEAST & POWER

1 CORINTHIANS 3:6 *I planted the seed, Apollos watered it, but God made it grow.*

 Activity

Directions

1. Mix yeast and 1 cup warm water.

2. Divide the yeast solution into 2 bowls.

3. Add flour to one bowl and grape juice to the other.

4. Use funnel to put each solution into a soda bottle and label the bottle.

5. Inflate and then deflate both balloons. Put a balloon over the mouth of the bottle and secure it with string so air cannot escape.

6. Shake the bottles. Lay the bottles on their sides.

7. Watch what happens.

Why it works: The carbon dioxide gas produced by the yeast causes the balloon to fill. It creates enough power to blow up the balloons.

 Talk about it

It is the yeast, the tiny living plants, that causes the mixture to rise and releases the power. In this case, the power blew up a balloon. God gives the power and causes the growth in us. Talk about things you may need to do but don't feel you have the strength. Pray together for God's power and strength.

DAY 3

UNDERSTANDING GOD'S POWER

ACTS 1:8 *But you will receive power when the Holy Spirit comes on you; and you will be my witnesses... to the ends of the earth.*

 Activity

Make balloon rockets. Cut a string to hang across a room. Slide the string through a 4 inch piece of straw. Tie or tape the ends of the string to each end of the room (tie to door handles or chairs). Pull the straw piece to one end of the string. Blow up a balloon and hold the end closed. Attach the balloon to the straw with a piece of tape, keeping the balloon opening toward the end of the room. Let go of the balloon and watch it travel across the room on the straw.

 Talk about it

The air in the balloon provided power to move the balloon like a rocket. When you let God and His Holy Spirit into your life you also receive power. With that power Jesus said you can witness to the world. What does it mean to witness? How can you witness now? Talk about God's power in contrast to man's power.

God Provides

*Happy is the family that knows God provides
for they will learn to laugh!*

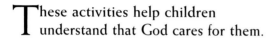

These activities help children
understand that God cares for them.

MATERIALS

❖ feathers
❖ basket or bowl
❖ sandal
❖ bread, roll, or crackers
❖ red paper
❖ scissors
❖ glue

Preparation

Place the sandal, feathers, and bread in the
basket or bowl.

DAY 1

ELIJAH AND THE RAVENS

1 KINGS 17:6 *The ravens brought him bread and
meat in the morning and bread and meat in the
evening, and he drank from the brook.*

 Activity 1

Look at the basket and talk about picnics. Would
anyone go on a picnic without food? Would you
take a trip and take nothing with you? God told
Elijah to go somewhere and not to take anything
with him. Take out the sandal.

 Talk about it

Discuss how Elijah obeyed God and went with
only the clothes he was wearing.

God told him that he would be provided for by
birds, by ravens. Take out the feather. How
much food could a bird carry? Would it be
enough to feed a grown-up? The birds brought
food twice a day. They brought bread and meat.

 Activity 2

Take out the bread. Have a bread picnic
remembering God can send help anywhere we
go. How does worry show a lack of trust in
God? We need to give God our cares and let
Him lighten our load. Let everyone share what
worries them, then pray together, giving the
worry to God.

DAY 2

FEATHER FUN

MATTHEW 6:26 *Look at the birds of the air; they do not sow or reap or store away in barns, and yet your heavenly Father feeds them. Are you not much more valuable then they?*

 Activity

Look at the feathers and pass them around. Are they light or heavy? Have a race blowing the feathers across a room.

 Talk about it

God knows that although birds must depend on Him for everything, they soar into the sky and make beautiful music. Our problems should not keep us from feeling light as a feather. We need to trust God to provide for our needs and to solve our problems. Share a prayer God answered. Blow the feathers to each other. Do they move easy? Can God move obstacles away as easily?

DAY 3

LETTING GOD PROVIDE

MATTHEW 6:33-34 *But seek first his kingdom and his righteousness, and all these things will be given to you as well. Therefore, do not worry about tomorrow, for tomorrow will worry about itself. Each day has enough trouble of its own.*

 Activity

Have each person cut out a paper heart. Glue a feather onto the heart.

 Talk about it

God wants our hearts to be happy. He loves us and will care for us. Let your feather heart be a reminder to give all your problems to God. Take time to talk about your needs and desires. Pray, giving all your needs and desires to God.

Seeking

Happy is the family that seeks the good in their children for they will be grateful!

Use these activities to help your children be grateful for blessings.

— MATERIALS —

❖ paper and pencil
❖ chairs
❖ scrap book or photo album
❖ scissors

THE LORD IS A BLESSING

PROVERBS 28:20 *A faithful man will be richly blessed...*

 Activity

This game needs to be played with at least 3 people. If there are only 2 people in the family, invite another family to participate.

Directions

1. One person is the caller. The caller stands in the middle.

2. The caller says out loud, "The Lord is a blessing to everyone who" and finishes the sentence with a description such as "has blue eyes" or "has children" or "knows the Savior".

3. Everyone fitting the description has to get up and find a new seat.

4. The caller also finds a seat.

5. The one person who does not get a seat is the new caller.

If the caller runs out of ideas take a minute or two to think of some blessings!!

 Talk about it

The object of the caller is to find blessings in the life of other people playing! We all need to be happy that God blesses others and rejoice with them!

DAY 2

ACROSTIC HUNT

PSALM 119:2 *Blessed are they who keep his statutes and seek him with all their heart.*

 Activity

Have a scavenger hunt to find the items in this list and then look at the message of the acrostic. The first letter of each word forms the message. Let each person copy the list, or divide into teams for a large family, and see who finds the most in 10 minutes or how quickly all the items can be collected!

- ○ Gold jewelry
- ○ Orange crayon
- ○ Dime
- ○ Ink pen
- ○ Stone
- ○ Burnt out light bulb
- ○ Old shoelace
- ○ Violet paper
- ○ Eight sticks

 Talk about it

Psalm 119 is a Hebrew acrostic. Each verse begins with a letter of the Hebrew alphabet, making it easier to memorize. An acrostic can be a puzzle in which the first letters of each word spell something. What do the first letters of the items in the hunt spell? The list did not appear to have anything in common at first glance. We don't always see what we have in common with others. But we do have a God who loves us. If we're hunting for heroes, it can be hard, but God tell us that those who seek the Lord with their heart are blessed. Name some heroes you want to be like.

A scavenger hunt can be exciting, racing to find things, even odd little items. We should get excited about discovering things about others, even odd little facts about them. Take time to discover something new about each family member!

DAY 3

SCRAP BOOKS AND MEMORIES

HEBREWS 13:7 *Remember your leaders, who spoke the word of God to you. Consider the outcome of their way of life and imitate their faith.*

 **Activity**

Look at family photos, albums or scrapbooks.

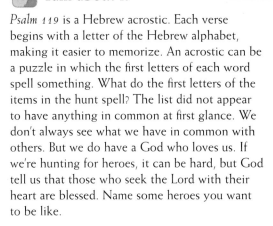 **Talk about it**

It can be fun to look back and reflect on the past. God sent people in our lives to teach us. Cut paper into heart shapes. Write or draw a picture of someone who taught you a lesson about God. On the back write something to remind you of the lesson learned. Put these papers in the family photo album.

Outdoors

Happy is the family that walks together for they will journey with the Lord.

U se these outdoor activities to understand how to walk with God and appreciate the world God made.

DAY 1

WALKING TOGETHER

EPHESIANS 5:15 *Therefore be careful how you walk, not as unwise men, but as wise [NASB].*

 Activity and discussion

Take a walk as a family.

Talk while walking. Did you know where you were walking? Did you watch for holes, rocks, and obstacles? Did you watch for traffic? Did anyone point out obstacles as you walked? Did you choose a safe place to walk? When we walk as Christians are there obstacles we need to consider?

Make stops at the three places noted and read the matching verses, discovering lessons in the Bible that relate to objects outdoors:

A LARGE TREE: *Matthew 13:34* Talk about how each tree starts as little seed but grows to an enormous size. God's kingdom keeps growing as more people believe in Jesus.

A LEAFY TREE: *John 3:8* Is there a breeze now that can be heard or felt? Can anyone see a leaf blowing in the wind? Can you see the wind? Blow on your hand. Can you feel the air as you blow it out? Can you see the Holy Spirit? Have you felt the power of the Spirit?

A LARGE ROCK: *Psalm 31:3* Let everyone share how God is like a rock. Rocks are strong. Caves are openings in rocks that give protection.

Talk about other creations you see and Bible stories related to them.

GOD'S WALK

DAY 3

STAR ACHIEVEMENTS

1 CORINTHIANS 15:41 *The sun has one kind of splendor, the moon another and the stars another; and star differs from star in splendor.*

 Activity

Go out on a clear night and look at the stars. Try counting the stars. See if you can find one of the constellations.

 Talk about it

God made the stars yet he made each star different. God made each person different too. Each person, like each star, has his or her own splendor. Think of things that makes each person light up and feel excited. Each person is a light for Christ but may shine in a different way. Talk about ways to be a light for Christ.

Notice how constellations form by drawing imaginary lines between stars in a cluster. The path in a life is an imaginary line connecting the events. How does walking with God keep a person on the right path?

DAY 2

HAVE A COOKOUT

JOHN 21:9 *When they landed, they saw a fire of burning coals there with fish on it, and some bread.*

 Activity

Have a cookout or picnic as a family. After eating read *John 21:4-14*. Discuss the cookout Jesus had with the disciples.

 Talk about it

Is it fun to have a picnic? How does the food taste? Do you think God wants you to have fun? Do you suppose God is concerned about your need for food and relaxation?

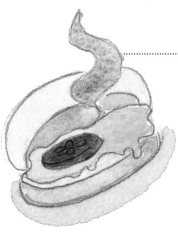

Seasonings

Happy is the family that values each child for they will become well-rounded individuals.

Use these activities to encourage your children's individuality.

— MATERIALS —

✧ *English muffins, or pizza dough*
✧ *pizza sauce*
✧ *toppings for pizza (mushrooms, meat, peppers, cheese)*
✧ *different seasonings and spices to smell*

DAY 1

MAKE MINI PIZZAS

1 CORINTHIANS 12:11 *All of these are the work of one and the same Spirit, and he gives them to each one, just as he determines.*

 Activity

Let everyone top off an English muffin (or a circle of pizza dough) with sauce, toppings, and cheese. If using pizza dough, roll dough and cut into 4 inch circles. Bake pizzas at 200°C (400°F), Gas Mark 6, till dough is cooked and cheese lightly browned. (English muffins can be toasted, then inserted in the microwave.)

 Talk about it

Did everyone enjoy the pizza? How did everyone decide what topping to put on their pizza? What does this say about individuality? God's word says the Holy Spirit chooses what gifts to give each person. How do you decide what gift to give someone? The recipient might give a hint but the giver makes the final decision. Thank God for the gifts you have received.

DAY 2

SEASONINGS

COLOSSIANS 4:6 *Let your conversation be always full of grace, seasoned with salt, so that you may know how to answer everyone.*

 Activity

Cover the names of the spices and seasonings. Let everyone smell the spices and seasonings, trying to guess the scents.

 Talk about it

Talk about how each seasoning is used. What happens if too much is used? A cook has to experiment to learn how much to add. Let everyone pick up a pinch of one spice. Discuss how the colors and textures differ.

Today's verse tells us to season our conversation with salt. How much salt is needed? Is bad language a Christian salt? Is gossip? Is preaching to others when asked a question like dumping a shaker of salt onto a little food?

 Bonus Activity

Make spiced apples. Peel, core, and slice the apples. Mix a pinch of cinnamon with a tablespoon of sugar and sprinkle on apples. Microwave three minutes, or cook over low heat

DAY 3

JESUS – A GOD FOR ALL PEOPLE

JOHN 3:16 *For God so loved the world that he gave his one and only Son, that whoever believes in him shall not perish but have eternal life.*

 Activity

List all the names you can think of for Jesus.

 Talk about it

What are some names for Jesus? Each person thinks of Jesus differently, often thinking about an attribute of God that is helpful to that person at that moment. Salt is used on many foods and used for many things other than flavoring food, such as preserving food, melting ice when slippery, and healing wounds.

 Talk about it

Talk about different nationalities of people that God made. Discuss how God loves each and every person no matter the color of skin or racial heritage.

Giving to Others

Happy is the family that knows that in giving we receive for they will be generous!

Use these activities to help your children learn to be generous and appreciate what God gives them.

— MATERIALS —

- ✧ pennies
- ✧ scale or make one with a ruler and a small block
- ✧ empty toilet paper roll
- ✧ construction paper
- ✧ glue or tape
- ✧ scissors
- ✧ little gifts (coins, candy, tiny toys, earrings)

DAY 1

GOD'S BALANCING SCALE

LUKE 21:3 *"I tell you the truth," he said, "this poor widow has put in more than all the others."*

 Activity

Place the ruler on the block, with center of ruler over center of the block. Use one finger to keep the ruler balanced. Place two pennies at each end then remove the finger from the center. Is the ruler balanced? Now add 6 more pennies at one end. Is it still balanced? Try one penny at one end and nine at the other end.

 Talk about it

God said the widow who gave two pennies gave the most. Did He use the same kind of scale? God asks people to share the money that He gives them. God says to keep 9 pennies and give one back to Him. That is called tithing. Is that balanced? God doesn't measure by counting or weighing but by what is in a heart.

DAY 2

ROCKETS TO GO

PSALM 31:19 *How great is your goodness, which you have stored up for those who fear you, which you bestow in the sight of men on those who take refuge in you.*

 Preparation

Fill toilet paper rolls with surprises for each child. Use candy, coins, or tiny toys, and verses written on slips of paper. Stuff ends with tissue paper. Cover the rolls with colored paper and decorate like a rocket. Add paper wings to the bottom. Make cones for the rockets' noses. Cut 4 inch circles of paper, cut out ¼ of the circle and overlap the ends to form a cone. Glue or tape the cone to each rocket.

 Activity

Fly a rocket to each child and let them open it to find the treasures.

Talk about it

The generosity of God. Is it exciting to receive a surprise? Where does everything, even money come from? Thank God for being so generous.

DAY 3

GIVING IT AWAY — BLAST OFF!

2 CORINTHIANS 9:7 *Each man should give what he has decided in his heart to give, not reluctantly or under compulsion, for God loves a cheerful giver.*

 Activity

Talk about ways to be generous. Decide on one giving project to do as a family that involves giving – then do it. One idea is to make rockets for other children, perhaps children at a homeless shelter.

 Talk about it

How does it feel to give to others? Think about little ways to be generous, such as giving smiles, hugs, and compliments to one another.

Music

Happy is the family that knows that joyful noise is music to the ears for they will be filled with merriment!

Use these activities to rejoice with music!

— MATERIALS —

❖ musical instruments or bells
❖ Christian tapes or CDs and a player

MUSICAL CELEBRATIONS IN THE BIBLE

COLOSSIANS 3:16 *Let the word of Christ dwell in you richly as you teach and admonish one another with all wisdom, and as you sing psalms, hymns, and spiritual songs with gratitude in your hearts to God.*

 Activity

Listen to a Christian song on a cassette or CD. Read the song of Miriam in *Exodus 15:21.*

 Talk about it

How can words in a song teach us? Why did Miriam sing about a horse and the sea. Does everyone know the story Miriam sang? If not, find out. It's in the Bible in *Exodus 14:26-31.* Moses also sang about God's triumph in *Exodus 15:1-19.* The written words tell a story, but the words of a song are easier to remember than memorizing scripture. Why? Songs have a melody, a rhythm that our heart responds to because our hearts beat in rhythms.

Sing to the Lord

DAY 2

A MUSICAL PARADE

PSALM 150:6 *Let everything that has breath praise the Lord. Praise the Lord.*

 Activity

Read *Psalm 150*. Notice all the types of instruments used to praise God. Make kitchen instruments from pots and pans. Use those and other instruments to have a praise parade. March with the instruments. King David led a parade after a victory. Read about this in *2 Samuel 6:14-15*.

 Talk about it

A parade is a celebration. Think of reasons to celebrate God. Talk about all the things God made and what he does. Let each person name a favorite sound.

DAY 3

RHYTHM

EPHESIANS 5:19 *Speak to one another with psalms, hymns, and spiritual songs. Sing and make music in your heart to the Lord.*

 Activity

Clap in time to music. Then make a clapping pattern and have others repeat the pattern.

 Talk about it

Your heart beats in a rhythm pattern. When excited or afraid the heart beats faster. During sleep the heart beats slower. A puppy that is used to the beat of the mother dog's heart will sleep better next to a ticking clock because of its rhythm. What kind of music can we make in our heart to the Lord? When we learn scriptures and repeat them, does that make music too?

In repeating a rhythm, we need to listen and follow the same beat. In life, we need to listen to God's Word to follow his timing.

God's Love

Happy is the family that knows that God's love colors our world for they will see beauty.

Make rainbow books of praise to reflect on God's love.

— MATERIALS —

✧ *construction paper in rainbow colors*
✧ *markers*
✧ *hole punch*
✧ *paper fasteners*
✧ *scissors*

A RAINBOW BOOK OF GOD'S LOVE

GENESIS 9:13 *I have set my rainbow in the clouds, and it will be the sign of the covenant between me and the earth.*

 Activity

Cut papers into 4.25 x 5.5 inch pieces. Layer the colors in the order of the rainbow: red, orange, yellow, green, blue, indigo, and violet. Overlap the pages so all the colors show. Turn over the group of pages and cut across the bottom of the top page. On the red paper draw a heart as a reminder of God's love.

 Talk about it

Discuss the rainbow and Noah's ark. Talk about how the rainbow in the sky reminds us of God's love. Talk about other things God did to show His love. Draw other symbols on the red page as reminders of God's love.

DAY 2

CENTERED IN CHRIST

REVELATIONS 4:3 *And the one who sat there had the appearance of jasper and carnelian. A rainbow, resembling an emerald, encircled the throne.*

 Activity

Draw symbols on the other pages as reminders of God and His promises.

○ Orange for the Holy Spirit's presence, seen as flaming tongues in *Acts* 2:3. Draw a flaming tongue.

○ Yellow for light. Jesus is the light of the world and we are to be lights, too. Read *John* 8:12 and *Matthew* 5:14. Draw a candle.

○ Green for our everlasting God. In *Hosea* 14:8 God describes himself as the evergreen tree, bearing fruit in all seasons. Draw a tree.

○ Blue for water. Jesus described himself as living water in *John* 4:10-15. Baptism is done with water. Draw someone being baptized, or a pool of water.

○ Indigo is a violet blue color. In Bible times violet was used for royalty. The mix of blue of the sky and violet of royalty reminds us God adopts each believer, under heaven, as His child, a royal child. Read *Galations* 3:26. Draw yourself.

○ Violet, a royal color, reminds us that Jesus is the King of Kings. Draw a crown.

 Talk about it

Discuss the colors and symbols used. Talk about other attributes of God that the colors make you think about.

DAY 3

GATHERING TOGETHER

JOHN 13:34 *A new command I give you: Love one another. As I have loved you, so you must love one another.*

 Activity

Layer the pages and use paper fasteners to put the pages together.

 Talk about it

The pages alone did not make the book. The pages needed to be held together. The same is true with the family and a community – people need something to hold them together. What did Jesus say we must do? How can love bring people together? The books don't stay together without a fastener. The fastener had to be put through the holes and then spread open to keep the pages together. God's love needs to go into open hearts that accept Jesus. Have you done this? Do you need to ask Jesus to come into your heart?

Bread Plate Activities

Happy is the family that makes a house a loving home for they will learn hospitality!

These activities center on hospitality and praying for God to bless your home.

DAY 1

FASTING

MATTHEW 4:2 *After fasting forty days and forty nights he was hungry.*

 Activity

Fast for one day or just one meal. Set aside the money that would have been spent for the meal and give it to the poor.

 Talk about it

Jesus fasted 40 days. Is it hard to miss a meal? Many people in the world die from hunger every day. When Jesus fasted, he spent the extra time in prayer. Take time to pray now, especially for hungry people.

Jesus sometimes ate at friends' homes. He ate with Zacchaeus (*Luke 19:1-7*) and with Mary and Martha (*Luke 10:38-42*).

DAY 2

PREPARING FOR ANGELS AND OTHER VISITORS

HEBREWS 13:2 *Do not forget to entertain strangers, for by so doing some people have entertained angels without knowing it.*

 Activity 1

Make sandwiches for a homeless shelter.

 Talk about it

Jesus said that when we feed the hungry we feed him. Read this in *Matthew* 25:37-40.

 Activity 2 and discussion

Bake bread that can be frozen. Slice and freeze the bread. When angels visited Abraham, he gave them bread that Sarah, his wife, had baked. In *Hebrews* 13:2 we read that in entertaining strangers, we may be entertaining angels. Can we think of a time when we may have entertained angels? When unexpected company visits, take the bread out of the freezer and serve it to the guests.

DAY 3

BREAD HOUSE BLESSINGS

PSALM 127:1 *Unless the Lord builds the house, its builders labor in vain... .*

 Activity

Decorate a slice of bread to look like a house. Cut a second slice of bread diagonally for the roof. Use peanut butter or jelly for windows, doors, and the roof.

 Talk about it

Jesus was born in a town called Bethlehem. He is the Bread of Life. The name Bethlehem means "house of bread." Is your house a home for the bread of life? Do you spend time as a family making Jesus feel welcome? What can you do? Take time to walk in each room and ask God to bless your home.

Light

*Happy is the family that keeps the light burning
for they will be fired up for the Lord!*

Use a candle to understand more fully what it means to be a light for Christ.

— MATERIALS —

❖ candle to fit inside a jar
❖ empty glass jar with a lid or cover
❖ small candle in a candle holder or on a cupcake, one for each person
❖ matches
❖ large candle
❖ sequins and pins

DAY 1

LIGHT NEEDS FUEL!

MATTHEW 5:15 *Neither do people light a lamp and put it under a bowl. Instead they put it on its stand, and it gives light to everyone in the house.*

 Activity

Take a candle and place it in a jar. Light the candle and the put a lid on the jar. Start reading by the candlelight. Read *Matthew 5:1-13.* If the candle is still lit start singing a song about light (This Little Light of Mine).

 Talk about it

Once the candlelight dies out, stop and ask why the candlelight cannot continue. Discuss how the candle ran out of oxygen. Can a Christian light grow dim or go out? What does it need to keep on burning? Uncover and relight the candle, set it on a stand or table, then finish reading the Bible passage or singing the song.

DAY 2

FAMILY CANDLE

MATTHEW 5:16 *In the same way, let your light shine before men, that they may see your good deeds and praise your Father in heaven.*

 Activity

Take a large candle and with pins and sequins decorate the candle. Add silk flowers with the pins (if desired). Use this candle to light and pray around for family times such as birthdays, devotions, holidays and anniversaries.

 Talk about it

How can you let your light shine? Can your family be a light for other families. End by lighting the candle and praying for God to help your family be a light for others.

DAY 3

PASSING THE LIGHT.

JOHN 1:9 *The true light that gives light to every man was coming into the world.*

 Activity

Give each person an unlit candle (this works best in a dark room). Now light one of the candles. Have the person with the lit candle light the next candle and pass on the light till each person's candle is lit. (Note, don't breath on the light or it will go out).

 Talk about it

Remind everyone that we must not only keep the light burning but we must share light with others. God's light is for everyone. Discuss how telling others about Jesus is a way to share God's light.

Hunting for Answers

Happy is the family that seeks good in others for they will find it!

These activities encourage children to discover good things in themselves and others.

— MATERIALS —

✧ *paper and pencil*
✧ *small individual treasures, gift wrapped*
✧ *concordance*

DAY 1

TREASURE HUNT

MATTHEW 7:8 *For everyone who asks receives; he who seeks finds; and to him who knocks, the door will be opened.*

 Preparation

Make individual treasure hunts for each family member. Choose 4 or 5 places to hide clues for each person's hunt. Cut papers shaped like slices of bread.

Write clues on the papers. Clues can be Bible verses to look up, secret codes, riddles, or pictures glued onto paper and cut into jigsaw puzzles. Hide clues and at the last location hide the small gift.

 Note

If children are old enough to help, let them draw a name and make up the clues for that person.

Note that each person's clues should have his or her name on them or be in a special color for them. This way no one takes the wrong clue by mistake.

 Activity

Give everyone their first clue. Some people may need hints to solve their clues. Wait for everyone to finish before opening the treasures!

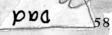

 ## Talk about it

To obtain the treasure in this hunt, the clues had to be followed and then the gift had to be opened. At any time a person could turn away and decide not to continue the hunt. We have to choose to follow Jesus to receive a heavenly treasure. Look up *John 6:51* for a treasure that will last forever.

The treasure hunt involved solving one clue at a time. Jesus takes us one day at a time, giving us what we need when we need it. Focus on God's kingdom and following God's will.

DAY 2

SCRIPTURE HUNT

ACTS 17:11 *Now the Bereans were of more noble character than the Thessalonians, for they received the message with great eagerness and examined the Scriptures every day to see if what Paul said was true.*

 ## Activity

Have available a concordance or a Bible containing a concordance. Discuss how to use a concordance. Then use it to find scriptures for the following topics: joy, sorrow, loneliness, healing. Add others to this list.

 ## Talk about it

Talk about how God has answers for all our needs and speaks to us through His Word. Discuss examples of how people you know model the Scriptures they read. Treasure hunts are exciting and challenging. Seeking God's will and answers for life provide challenges with great rewards! Have everyone share something they discovered today!

DAY 3

ANSWERS FOR A LIFETIME:

MATTHEW 7:7 *Ask and it will be given to you; seek and you will find; knock and the door will be opened to you.*

 ## Activity

Buy or create a small journal. Using these journals draw the path you traveled in your life. Add valleys, hills, meeting God, and new people. Include treasures discovered along the way.

 ## Talk about it

Share your paths with one another and talk about how God provided and answered needs and prayers. Note that the verse for today is almost the same as the first one read this week. It's important to remember that God has the answers. Jesus emphasizes this by repeating His words again.

In God's Image

*Happy is the family who knows each child is
a gift from God for they will rejoice!*

Help children know they are special
to God with these activities.

— MATERIALS —

✧ *a small wrapped gift for each child
(candy, book, trinket)*
✧ *a shoe box*
✧ *magazines*
✧ *scissors*
✧ *glue*
✧ *mirror that can be glued inside shoe box*

DAY 1

SPECIAL EDITION

PSALM 127:3 *Sons are a heritage from the Lord,
children are a reward from him.*

 Activity

Read the verse and talk about how each member
of the family was chosen. How did mom and
dad meet? Let each parent talk about the first
time they saw each child.

Pass out the gifts. Guess what's inside. Isn't it
exciting to receive a surprise gift? Open them
up. Thank God for the gift of life and for the
small gifts, too.

Talk about it

Talk about the importance of life and who is in
charge of life. Children are not like a gift that
can be returned or exchanged. Gifts from God
are rewards, not punishments or inconveniences.

Let everyone tell why each person in their
family is special to them. How did God make
them special? (*Note: Some parents may wish to touch
on the meaning and implications of abortion.*)

DAY 2

CREATION BOX

GENESIS 1:27 *So God created man in his own image, in the image of God he created him; male and female he created them.*

 Preparation

Glue a mirror inside the shoe box. Replace the cover.

 Activity

Talk about all that God made and gave us. Cut out pictures of creation and glue them on the outside of the box. Cut out bread, grapes, and a cross as a reminder that God gave us His son, Jesus.

 Talk about it

God made so many things. Use the box as a reminder to pray for all that God created. Ask what God made that was the best, the most special creation. Let each person peek inside, one at a time, and see what God loves most!

DAY 3

IT'S WHAT'S INSIDE THAT COUNTS!

1 CORINTHIANS 15:45 *So also it is written, "The first man, Adam, became a living being" the last Adam, a life-giving spirit.*

 Activity

Fill the shoe box by writing down on slips of paper things to do for God. Or as a reminder of special blessings from God to your family insert sea shells from a day at the beach, a photo from a family trip or other memorable items.

 Talk about it

God created human beings and allowed them to choose what to do – to sin or obey God. We, too, can choose. We are created for good but we must make a choice between doing right and doing wrong. Just as we fill the box, we have the choice of what to put in our hearts and our lives.

Discernment

*Happy is the family that discerns truth for
they will make wise choices.*

These activities help children learn
to sort things out in making
decisions.

— MATERIALS —

✧ basin of water
✧ objects which float
✧ objects which sink
✧ magnet
✧ magnetic objects
✧ non-magnetic objects

DAY 1

ATTRACTION

MATTHEW 13:30 *Let both grow together until the
harvest. At that time I will tell the harvesters: "First
collect the weeds and tie them in bundles to be burned;
then gather the wheat and bring it into my barn."*

 Activity

Place magnetic and non-magnetic objects on a
table. Guess which ones will be magnetic. Then
check and sort the objects into piles of magnetic
and non-magnetic objects. The objects drawn to
the magnet have iron in them.

 Talk about it

The iron in the materials attracts certain objects
to the magnet. Other objects look similar; they
look like they will be drawn to the magnet but
are not. Why are some drawn to the magnet and
others are not?

Jesus talks about sorting weeds and wheat. The
tares look like the wheat as young plants but
when the harvest comes, it is easy to tell them
apart. God will know how to sort people
according to what is inside them.

DAY 2

SINK OR SWIM

MATTHEW 14:29 *"Come," he said. Then Peter got down out of the boat, walked on the water and came toward Jesus.*

 Activity

Testing for buoyancy

Procedure:

1. Fill a basin with water.

2. Decide which objects might float or sink and test them in the water.

3. Make separate piles for the objects that float and the objects that sink.

4. Put a pebble on a floating object. Does it still sink?

 Talk about it

We can use the water to separate the objects. But water can change. It can be solid like ice, a gas like vapor or steam, or it can be a liquid. Peter walked on the water (a miracle), but sank when he took his eyes off of Christ. Peter asked Christ for help. We can do impossible things with the help of Christ. Trusting Jesus is like learning to swim. The water will hold us up if we learn to trust it. Is it harder learning to swim or learning to trust Jesus?

DAY 3

CHOICES

MATTHEW 25:32 *And all the nations will be gathered before him; and he will separate the people from one another as a shepherd separates the sheep from the goats.*

 Activity

Read *Matthew 13:24-30, 36-43*

 Talk about it

Discuss the scripture reading. Can Jesus tell the evil from the righteous? How? Does God see what we do or why we do it? What does He see in our hearts? How can we decide what is good or what is evil? Is it hard when we listen to others? Who should we ask when we are confused? How can we look at Jesus and understand how He would decide?

 Try it

Let each person think of a decision they need to make, or think of a family decision to be made. List benefits and problems of each choice. Think of any parable or Bible person involved in a similar choice. Then pray about it.

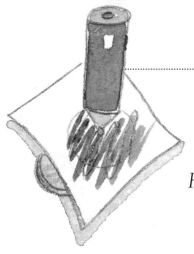

Impressions

*Happy is the family that knows impressions last
for they will strive to imitate Christ.*

Enjoy learning how objects leave impressions and use that as a bridge to understanding how people also leave impressions.

— MATERIALS —

✧ crayons
✧ various objects for paper rubbing
✧ paper
✧ knife for soap or wood carving
✧ birth certificate
✧ candle and a wax seal (or use a coin)

DAY 1

CRAYON RUBBINGS

PROVERBS 27:17 *As iron sharpens iron, so one man sharpens another.*

Activity

Place paper over various objects and rub the crayon over the paper. The crayon will show the outline of the object, texture, and some details.

Talk about it

The paper rubbing took on some of the looks of the actual object. Rubbing a crayon over a coin can reveal the picture on the coin, the denomination, and sometimes the words. They rub off!

What happens when we spend a lot of time with someone? Do children who play together use many of the same phrases or words? Do friends start becoming alike in attitudes and in other ways? Do you want to be like someone you know or admire? Do you try to be like Jesus? Do you spend enough time with Jesus to be like Him?

DAY 2

ENGRAVINGS

HEBREWS 10:16 *This is the covenant I will make with them after that time, says the Lord. I will put my laws in their hearts, and I will write them on their minds.*

 Activity

If available, examine something engraved. Using a knife, carve something onto a piece of wood or bar of soap.

 Talk about it

Something engraved cannot be removed without ruining what it is engraved on. It is permanent. What is written on your heart?

DAY 3

WHAT DO PEOPLE SEE IN US?

EPHESIANS 1:13 *And you also were included in Christ when you heard the word of truth, the gospel of your salvation. Having believed, you were marked in him with a seal, the promised Holy Spirit,*

 Activity

Look at a birth certificate. To be authentic it must have a seal on it, the impression made from an official stamp of the county, state, or country where a person is born. Touch the seal and feel it.

 Talk about it

People should see or feel a difference in the presence of a Christian. God sets His seal on believers.

 Activity

Light a candle and let the wax drip onto a piece of paper. Then press a seal into the wax to leave the design. If you don't have a seal, press a coin onto the wax. A cold candle is hard and does not take a seal, but soft wax does. Can the word of truth and love soften us so that God can put His seal on us?

Trinity

Happy is the family that knows there's a great depth to God for they will learn the fear of the Lord.

These activities help children discover truths about God.

— MATERIALS —

✧ *crayon and paper*
✧ *bandage*
✧ *cracker*
✧ *basket*
✧ *apple*
✧ *paring knife*
✧ *paint*

DAY 1

BASKET LESSON OF THE TRINITY

MATTHEW 3:16-17 *As soon as Jesus was baptized, he went up out of the water. At that moment heaven was opened, and he saw the Spirit of God descending like a dove and lighting on him. And a voice from heaven said, "This is my Son, whom I love; with him I am well pleased."*

 Activity

Set a basket (with a bandage, a crayon with paper and a cracker in it) on the table. Talk about how this one basket holds three different objects in it. There is one God but three distinct persons of the Trinity. Talk about each object and how that object reminds us of one person of the Trinity. Look up these verses for each object:

○ A bandage for the Holy Spirit as our comforter *(Acts 9:31)*.

○ A crayon and paper for Our Father and Creator *(Hebrews 11:3)*.

○ A cracker for Jesus – the Bread of Life *(John 6:35)*.

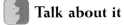 **Talk about it**

Read *Mark 1:9-11* and notice the presence of the Trinity. Talk about what each person of the Trinity means and how that gives us a better understanding of God.

DAY 2

CUTTING APPLES

ISAIAH 40:26 *Lift your eyes and look to the heavens: Who created all these? He who brings out the starry host one by one, and calls them by name. Because of his great power and strength not one of them is missing.*

 Activity

Cut an apple crosswise to see a five pointed star of seeds.

 Talk about it

God created the apple with a shiny skin to protect the food inside. God the Father protects us. The food, like Jesus, the bread of life, nourishes us. Inside the apple, are seeds. The seeds, like the Holy Spirit, bring new growth, producing more fruit. It is through the seeds, that the apples are multiplied. It was through receiving the Holy Spirit, that people became Christians.

Some people say the star represents the wounds of Jesus. As people get to know us, they will see the star qualities of Jesus in us.

DAY 3

APPLE PRINTS

EPHESIANS 3:19 *And to know this love that surpasses knowledge – that you may be filled to the measure of all the fullness of God.*

 Activity

Cut open apples crosswise and dip them in paint. Then stamp them on paper to make apple prints. You can see the outer shape of the apple, the inner shape, and the star formed by the seeds. The 3 parts remind us that God includes the three persons, Father, Son, and Holy Spirit. They are all united in one.

 Talk about it

How does the painting look? Can you tell the real thing from looking at the painting? It isn't three dimensional anymore but it leaves a picture of one slice of the apple. We only understand a little about the Trinity. Imagine if you never saw a real apple but only the print of the cut apple – could you sense how it tastes? Could you picture how it looks? The same is true with the Triune God, we don't see everything. Only in heaven will we fully understand God and the Trinity. Read *Ephesians 3:14-19* and discover that there will always be more to learn about God.

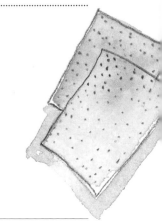

Decision-making

Happy is the family that lets children make decisions for they will be leaders.

These activities help children understand that decision-making is a choice, and people who make wise choices make good leaders.

— MATERIALS —

✢ sandpaper
✢ acrylic paint
✢ rocks
✢ paintbrush

DAY 1

HOUSES AND FOUNDATIONS OF SAND

MATTHEW 7:26 *And everyone who hears these words of mine, and does not put them into practice is like a foolish man who built his house on sand.*

 Activity

Paint a house on sandpaper. Let it dry. Then run it under water.

Talk about it

The paint was on the sand and the sand washed away, taking the paint away too. Try painting the sandpaper again. Rub the painted sandpaper on wood. Again, the paint will come off. Sand is not solid but made up of individual grains. As a result, there is not enough unity for the house. Why is sand a poor foundation for houses? What did Jesus mean when he compared a foolish builder to a person who hears God's words and does not act upon them?

DAY 2

FOUNDATION OF ROCK

MATTHEW 7:24-25 *Therefore, everyone who hears these words of mine, and puts them into practice is like a wise man who built his house on the rock. The rain came down, the streams rose, and the winds blew, and beat against that house; yet it did not fall, because it had its foundation on the rock.*

 Activity and discussion

Use the same paints to paint a house on a rock. Let it dry. Pour water over it. The paint remains. The rock is solid and doesn't fall apart or wash away so the house remains firmly painted on the rock. A house built on solid rock has a good foundation that stands against storms. What did Jesus mean when He said that people who listen to and act on God's Word are like a wise builder? What words have you heard and acted on?

DAY 3

LEADERSHIP

PSALM 32:8 *I will instruct you and teach you in the way which you should go; I will counsel you and watch over you.*

 Preparation

Hide a treat somewhere out of sight.

 Activity

Ask your children to find the hidden treat. If they don't succeed, give poor instructions. Then if needed, give good instructions.

 Talk about it

A good leader gives good instructions. A good follower obeys the instructions. When this happens, good things happen and things go well. Talk about a good leader. Take turns leading "follow-the-leader" games. Discuss how the leader needs to understand what the followers can do. If a leader is tiny and crawls under a chair, some bigger people may not be able to follow.

Storytelling

Happy is the family that listens for they will learn to accept one another.

These activities help children understand the importance of giving correct information although each person's perspective gives them different memories and a unique story.

— MATERIALS —

✧ family album or photos of a family event
✧ paper and pencil

The Parable of the growing seed
He also....., this is.....
the kingdom of..... is
like. A..... scatters....
on the...... Night
and..... whether

Matthew 13:1-23

DAY 1

STORY JUMBLE

1 CORINTHIANS 14:33 *For God is not a God of disorder but of peace, as in all the congregations of the saints.*

 Preparation

Copy a familiar Bible parable, leaving blank spaces for several words: nouns, verbs, names, adjectives, etc.

 Activity

Ask family members to give a word for each blank, telling them what type of word you need (name, verb, etc.). Read the parable with the substitute words. See if anyone can recognize the real parable. Compare the real parable meaning to the jumbled story.

 Talk about it

How do words change the story? Is the story still true with new words? 2 Timothy 2:15 tells us to handle the word of God accurately. Discuss what this scripture verse means.

DAY 2

JUST THE FACTS!

ACTS 18:28 *For he [Paul] vigorously refuted the Jews in public debate, proving from the scriptures that Jesus was the Christ.*

 Activity

Have everyone open their Bible to the pre-selected parable (Matthew 13:1-23). Let one person read it. Then ask the six interrogative questions about the parable: Who was the story about? What happened? Why did someone tell the story? When or at what time of day or year did it take place? Where did it take place? How can we learn from the story?

 Talk about it

Discuss why it's important to understand the facts before making decisions. Discuss times when people need to know facts before making a decision.

DAY 3

REMEMBERING

HEBREWS 11:2 *For by it [faith] men of old gained approval.*

 Activity 1

Take out a family album and look at one photo event together. Let each person tell what they remember from the event. Write about the pictures as a family, writing the facts and adding comments from each person.

 Activity 2

Let each person tell his earliest memory of hearing about Jesus, using the 5 "W"s and "How." questions.

 Talk about it

Does everyone remember the same things? Do people have different memories as well as shared impressions of the same event? Does each person have a shared memory about Jesus? A different memory about Jesus?

Compare the same event told in two different gospels, such as the birth of Christ in *Luke 2:1-20* and *Matthew 1:18-12*.

Read *Hebrews 11* (called the Hall of Faith) to discover about past Bible heroes and heroines.

Prayer Connections

Happy is the family that knows children need the right power for they will plug into eternal power!

H elp your family tap into the power of prayer through these activities.

— MATERIALS —

✧ *flashlight with good batteries*
✧ *matches*
✧ *container of water*
✧ *pennies*

POWER SOURCES

MATTHEW 21:22 *If you believe, you will receive whatever you ask for in prayer.*

 Preparation

Unplug lamps or remove light bulbs from all the lights in a room. Have available flashlights with the good batteries removed.

 Activity

Have a nighttime devotional. Go into a dark room and ask someone to turn on a light and read from the Bible. When they can't turn on the light, tell them you know the light bulbs work and the power is on. Ask them to find one of the good flashlights informing them that the batteries work. Ask if they know the problem. Light a match and see if they can discover the problem. Fix the problems then read the Bible verse.

 Talk about it

Talk about how power sources are useful but only when they are plugged in with working lightbulbs or the batteries are inserted in the flashlights.

DAY 2

HIT OR MISS

JAMES 4:2-3 *You do not have, because you do not ask God. When you ask, you do not receive, because you ask with wrong motives, that you may spend what you get on your pleasures.*

 Activity

Set a container with water on the ground. Give everyone five (5) pennies for tossing into the container and mark a line to stand behind. Blindfold each person, give them a spin, then see how many pennies they get in. They will hear a splash if they succeed. Remove the blindfold and let the person try again with 5 coins. Give everyone a turn.

 Talk about it

Is it hard to hit a target you can't see? Is it hard to find your way when blindfolded? Is it hard to get prayer answers if you don't look to God? How does wrong doing and sin blind us to God's power?

DAY 3

POWERED UP WITH POW-WOW'S

MATTHEW 18:19 *Again I tell you that if two of you on earth agree about anything you ask for, it will be done for you by my Father in heaven.*

 Activity

A POW-WOW is an acronym for Pray Over Worry and Worship Over Wonders! Write down the pow-wows of each person. Let each person tell his biggest worry and best wonder. Form a prayer circle, holding hands. Let each person pray for the person to his right, with a one sentence prayer for the worry and a one sentence thanks for the wonder.

 Talk about it

How does it feel to share worries and joys and to let someone else pray for you? When you let someone else pray for you it helps release the worry to God. Praying for others helps you understand them better.

Enlightened!

Happy is the family that knows there is more happening in a child's mind than we see for the family will lift up the children in prayer!

Rejoice as you understand how your child thinks and sees the world. Pray for God's wisdom, for He knows their thoughts.

— MATERIALS —

- ✧ pennies
- ✧ white grape juice
- ✧ small container
- ✧ white paper
- ✧ small paintbrush

DAY 1

CLEANING WITH WHITE GRAPE JUICE

1 JOHN 1:7 *But if we walk in the light as he is in the light, we have fellowship with one another, and the blood of Jesus, his Son purifies us from all sin.*

 Activity

Place the dirty pennies in a container of grape juice. Watch the pennies come clean! The ones that are the dirtiest will take longer.

 Why it works

The copper reacts and combines with the air to form copper oxides. This is why they're dirty. The juice contains acids which break down the copper oxides and frees the copper to make them clean.

 Talk about it

It does not seem possible to use grape juice to clean yet the acid in it has the ability to clean. In the Good Samaritan parable, the Samaritan used wine, made from grapes, to clean the wounds of the hurt man. Likewise, it doesn't seem possible that blood cleanses, yet we are cleansed by the blood of Jesus.

DAY 2

INVISIBLE MESSAGES

1 CORINTHIANS 13:12 *Now we see but a poor reflection as in a mirror; then we shall see face to face. Now I know in part; then I shall know fully, even as I am fully known.*

 Activity

Use a paintbrush and grape juice to write a message on paper. Let the paper dry. The message is invisible. Now heat the paper with an iron or hold it an inch above a flame. The message appears. Write messages to each other!

 Why it Works

The juice contains carbon compounds. When heated the compounds break down and separate out the carbon. Black carbon reveals the message.

 Talk about it

White grape juice looks similar to water yet it contains much that is hidden. People have hidden qualities, too. The warmth of God's love helps other people see hidden qualities of joy, peace, and love. God sees all, even the blackness of sins that we often attempt to hide from people.

DAY 3

ENLIGHTENED

EPHESIANS 5:13 *But everything exposed by the light becomes visible.*

 Activity

Talk to each other. Listen to each person and see how many new things you can discover: other's interests, things they did that you never knew, or the person's dreams and hopes.

 Talk about it

Our minds are enlightened as we discover more and more about one another and ourselves.

Shadow Puppets

Happy is the family that knows fear comes from lack of enlightenment for they will walk in the light

Have fun learning that shadows form when objects block light and how we need to let God's light shine.

— MATERIALS —

✧ black paper
✧ flashlight
✧ 2 craft sticks
✧ scissors
✧ clear tape

DAY 1

LIGHTS AND SHADOWS

LUKE 8:16 *Now no one lights a lamp and hides it in a jar or puts it under a bed. Instead he puts in on a stand, so that those who come in can see the light.*

 Activity

Use a flashlight and objects from around the house to cast shadows in a dark room. Let children try to guess each object. Then shine the second flashlight on the objects to reveal them.

 Talk about it

A shadow forms when objects block the light. A simple object can appear to be a scary monster till the light reveals the real object. We feel afraid when we see danger but the way out of danger is blocked. Likewise, we need to trust someone who can see. We need to trust Jesus, who is the light.

DAY 2

MAKING A DRAGON SHADOW PUPPET.

LUKE 8:17 *For there is nothing hidden that will not be disclosed, and nothing concealed that will not be known or brought out into the open.*

 Activity

Cut a dragon head out of black paper. Tape it to a stick. Cut the candle and tape it to a stick. Use a flashlight to make the dragon and candle shadows.

 Talk about it

Making shadow puppets is fun because we know they are not real. In life we need to seek the light and the truth so we won't be afraid. The Bible is true. Talk about the difference between hiding and concealing the truth and surprises.

DAY 3

PUPPET SHOW

JAMES 1:17 *Every good and perfect gift is from above, coming down from the Father of the heavenly lights, who does not change like shifting shadows.*

 Activity

Shine light on the dragon in a dark room for a dragon shadow. Tell the mini-story below and use the candle to cover the dragon towards the end of the story.

 Story

Once a little child hid under layers and layers of blankets. He was sure a dragon lurked in the room, spitting fire and waiting to burn him. His parents told him there was no dragon but he felt sure about what he saw in the dark. He pointed out the dragon that he saw. His parents prayed and prayer helped melt the dragon. The boy peeked out from under the covers and saw only a candle glowing where he'd seen the dragon.

Understanding

Happy is the family that knows knowledge brings understanding for they will be wise.

Let these activities inspire your family to explore the Bible.

— MATERIALS —

✧ paper
✧ pencils
✧ magnifying glass
✧ dictionary
✧ small objects related to Bible stories

DAY 1

MEMORY ON TRAYS

JOHN 14:26 *But the Counselor, the Holy Spirit, whom the Father will send in my name, will teach you all things and will remind you of everything I have said to you.*

 Preparation

Fill a tray with objects related to a Bible story, such as all types of toy animals, a toy boat, and tools for the story of Noah. Cover the tray.

 Activity

Uncover the tray and give everyone one minute to study the items. Cover the tray and let people write or draw all they remember seeing on the tray. Young ones can be paired with adults. See who remembers the most. Discuss the Bible stories depicted by the items. Use the items to retell the stories.

 Talk about it

God sent the Holy Spirit to help us remember His Word. How does remembering Bible verses help a person?

boat
fish
ring
spices

DAY 2

I MET THE BREAD MAKER

1 PETER 2:21 *To this you were called, because Christ suffered for you, leaving you an example, that you should follow in his steps.*

 Activity

Take turns pantomiming actions of Jesus or his disciples. Do this with partners if possible. See who guesses correctly.

Examples to pantomime: Jesus heals a blind man, Jesus heals a lame man, Peter catching no fish until Jesus tells him to let down his nets on the other side of the boat.

 Talk about it

To follow Jesus we have to know what he did. How do we find out? When we pantomime we need to think about the movements that show what happened. Similarly, when we do things we need to think about how others see our actions.

DAY 3

EXAMINING THE WORDS

JAMES 1:5 *If any of you lacks wisdom, he should ask God, who gives generously to all without finding fault, and it will be given to him.*

 Activity

Use a magnifying glass to show a Bible verse. Does that help people understand it better? Use a dictionary or Bible dictionary to look up tough works like "repent" or "synagogue".

 Talk about it

Does enlarging words, especially if you can't read, help with understanding? Knowing the meanings of words helps but that still may not make a verse clear. Talk about the meaning of Bible verses and how we can understand them. How do we get wisdom?

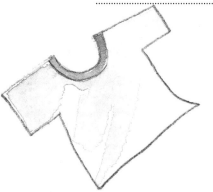

Family T's

Happy is the family that strives for unity of purpose for they will be loyal.

Developing team spirit unites families and encourages children to work as a team and give more effort to helping the team.

— MATERIALS —

❖ *plain T-shirts*
❖ *permanent markers or fabric paints*
❖ *paper and crayons*

DESIGNING FAMILY T-SHIRTS

EPHESIANS 3:14-15 *I kneel before the Father from whom his whole family in heaven and on derives its name.*

Activity

Design a family crest or coat of arms to put on a T-shirt. Include the family names on it. You might do an acrostic of your last name (each letter is the first letter of a word) and use Christian symbols or a picture that depicts something about your family, such as a shared hobby or something about where you live. Let everyone give ideas for this crest.

Talk about it

God designed families including your family. Even your family name is a gift from God. Talk about your family name, what language it came from and anything of its history that is known. Talk about names for God and God's people.

DAY 2

DECORATING FAMILY T-SHIRTS

MATTHEW 7:20 *Thus by their fruit you will recognize them.*

 Activity

Decorate T-shirts for each person with the design created as your family crest. Decide to place this on the front or the back. Let the children color in the designs. Help in decorating each other's shirt, using everyone's talents.

 Talk about it

When you go places together people will notice your shirts and the designs. What else do people notice when your family is together? What can your family do to produce fruits of love, joy, kindness and other spiritual fruits?

DAY 3

WEARING THE T'S

PHILIPPIANS 2:2 *... make my joy complete by being like-minded, having the same love, being one in spirit and purpose.*

 Activity

Wear your shirts and go for a walk together or serve others together. Stop by a neighbor's to say hello, help at a homeless shelter, or visit a nursing home. Always share God's love with those you meet.

 Talk about it

How does it feel to dress alike? How does it feel to do something together as a family? Can family members be alike on the inside – sharing the same love, spirit, and purpose? Does your family have set goals? If not, set a family goal now.

Working Together

Happy is the family that knows cooperation helps people reach a common goal for they will learn to share.

In these activities everyone works together and discovers fun in sharing.

— MATERIALS —

✧ paper, pencil, scissors
✧ large sheets of paper
✧ treasure

DAY 1

COOPERATIVE TREASURE HUNT

1 PETER 4:10 *Each one should use whatever gift he has received to serve others faithfully, administering God's grace in its various forms.*

 Preparation

Hide a treasure (something special that will be enjoyed), such as movie tickets or dessert. Use a Bible concordance to write scripture clues for the location. For example, hide the clue in a basket (*Acts 9:25*) in an upper room (*Luke 22:12*) under a bed (*Mark 4:21* or *Luke 11:7*). Write at least one clue for each family member. Hide the clues around a room.

 Activity

Have everyone share the one clue together to discover the treasure's location. Enjoy the treasure jointly or save it to share later.

 Talk about it

Cooperating made finding the treasure easier. Discuss how sharing chores, such as helping with dinner, unites a family and uses everyone's talents.

DAY 2

FAMILY KNOT

ROMANS 12:4 *Just as each of us has one body with many members, and these members do not all have the same function, ...*

 Activity

Stand in a circle: Place one hand inside the circle and grab hold of someone else's hand. Place the remaining hands in the circle and grab the hand of a different person. (Small families, invite another family to do this). This formed a family knot. Without letting go of any hands untangle yourselves to form a circle.

 Talk about it

How did you cooperate to become untangled? Who gave directions and who followed advice? Did you get more tangled at first? Did people have to climb over and under one another? When family problems and knots show up, how can you cooperate to solve them? It takes cooperation with people using different talents of leadership, creative ideas, and organizational skills to solve problems and knots. How are you going to help solve family knots when they occur?

DAY 3

MEMORY VERSE RACES

EPHESIANS 4:16 *From him the whole body, joined and held together by every supporting ligament, grows and builds itself up in love, as each part does its work.*

 Preparation

Write Bible verses, in large letters, on large sheets of paper. Cut the verses into jigsaw puzzles, cutting all into the same number of pieces. Make several puzzles. (For extra fun hide one piece from each puzzle)

 Activity

See which person or team completes a puzzle first. Did anyone have a problem with a missing piece? Let them search and find the piece.

 Talk about it

Jigsaw puzzles have to be fitted together. One piece missing leaves it incomplete. How does your family fit together? Is Jesus in the center?

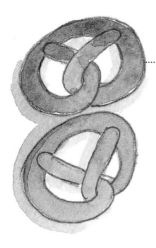

Pretzels

Happy is the family that knows prayer enfolds us in God's loving arms for they will have peace!

H elping children discover that prayer connects them to a loving God equips them for life!

— MATERIALS —

✧ *flour*
✧ *cooking oil*
✧ *coarse salt*
✧ *sugar*
✧ *1 package dry yeast*
✧ *margarine or an egg*
✧ *baking pan*
✧ *mixing bowl and spoon*
✧ *sauces or melted chocolate for dipping pretzels*

DAY 1

MAKING PRETZELS

LUKE 11:1 *One day Jesus was praying in a certain place. When he finished, one of His disciples said to him, "Lord teach us to pray just as John taught his disciples."*

 Activity

Make pretzels. Directions: Dissolve yeast in 1½ cups of warm water for 10 minutes. Add ½ tbsp sugar. Mix in 4 cups of flour and knead to form a soft dough. Pull off pieces of dough and roll into ropes. Shape into traditional pretzels or other designs. Place on a cookie sheet. Bake at 200°C (400°F), Gas Mark 6, for 15 minutes. Makes 2-4 dozen pretzels. Save some for the next day's activity.

 Talk about it

The traditional pretzel is shaped like arms folded in prayer. To make them you need a recipe and the right ingredients. What is needed to pray? Discuss Jesus' answer in *Luke 11:2-4*.

DAY 3

ENFOLDED IN LOVE

MARK 10:16 *And he took the children in his arms, put his hands on them, and blessed them.*

 Activity

Hug your children, then form a big group hug. Form a circle and give the person in front of you a back/shoulder rub. Turn around and repeat.

 Talk about it

The pretzel shape reminds us that Jesus enfolded in His arms the children whom the disciples tried to push away. He wraps each of us in His love. How does it feel to be hugged? Touched? Share a time when you really needed a hug.

DAY 2

EATING PRETZELS & PRAYER

LUKE 11:3 *Give us each day our daily bread.*

 Activity

Warm the pretzels and serve with sauces and dips. Try a favorite spaghetti sauce, melted cheese, melted chocolate, or various other dips.

 Talk about it

Basic pretzels can be enjoyed in lots of ways. Jesus called Himself the Bread of Life. What did He mean? Are there lots of ways to enjoy the presence of Jesus? When we ask for daily bread in the Lord's prayer are we also asking for Jesus? Are there lots of ways to pray?

Appearance

Happy is the family that looks beyond appearance for they will make friends.

Help your children look beyond outward appearance to discover beauty within people.

— MATERIALS —

✧ *black scarf or shawl (or black fabric)*
✧ *a robe*
✧ *a cane or stick for a staff*
✧ *small jar or near empty cooking oil bottle*
✧ *sticks*
✧ *an empty wallet (or with one dollar)*

DAY 1

COSTUMES

1 PETER 3:4 *Instead, it should be that of your inner self, the unfading beauty of a gentle and quiet spirit, which is of great worth in God's sight.*

 Activity

Have the children put on a scarf and robe. Take turns using the black scarf in a different way, as a costume part (i.e. around the shoulders and hunched up as an old woman, draped as a young woman going to a ball, or around the neck and down the front as a judge).

Talk about it

Clothes and costumes change and disguise our appearance. Clothes can protect us but also hide us. Do they change the person on the inside?

DAY 2

ELISHA AND WIDOW

2 KINGS 4:2 *Elisha replied to her, "How can I help you? Tell me, what do you have in your house?" "Your servant has nothing there at all," she said, "except a little oil."*

 Activity

Read 2 *Kings* 4:3-7 to find out what Elisha did with the oil. Hold up the wallet and say "Let's do something with the money in here." Let the children look inside and think about what they can do.

 Talk about it

Is having no money a problem? Make a list of things that people can do for free. Choose one thing to do together from the list and plan a time for it. The wallet was simply a prop. It made people think of money but without money things for free can be fun. Why? Because they are done with love and togetherness.

Go for a walk
visit Aunt Anne

DAY 3

A DIFFERENT PERSPECTIVE

COLOSSIANS 3:12 *Therefore as God's chosen people, holy and dearly beloved, clothe yourselves with compassion, kindness, humility, gentleness, and patience.*

 Activity

Read the story of the poor widow and the prophet Elijah found in *1 Kings* 17:9-24. Act it out, but do so from the perspective of the young son. In scene one let the mother ask the son for the oil. He discovers it is empty so she can't make her bread. She tells him to wait. (Let the son look out the window after she exits.) Tell about Elijah coming and his mother gathering sticks. The boy shows excitement when his mother runs in. She sends him for jars and then he watches her as she fills the jars. Now try thinking of scene two where the son dies and Elijah brings him back to life.

 Talk about it

Does the story bring out new ideas when seen from a different character? When we look with our eyes we see one thing but when we look with a new heart, the heart of Christ, we see things from a different perspective.

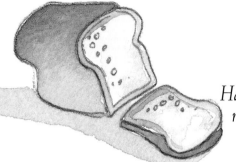

Money

*Happy is the family that knows what
really counts for they will prosper!*

Use these activities to discuss money,
saving, and spending wisely.

— MATERIALS —

- ❖ 3 cups flour
- ❖ 2 eggs
- ❖ ¼ cup warm water
- ❖ 3 tbsp sugar
- ❖ ¼ cup warm milk
- ❖ 1 packag yeast
- ❖ 1 teas salt
- ❖ ½ cup butter
- ❖ hot dogs
- ❖ barbecue sauce
- ❖ pennies or other coins

DAY 1

RISING DOUGH AND MAKING BREAD

MATTHEW 13:33 *He told them still another
parable: "The kingdom of heaven is like yeast that a
woman took and mixed into a large amount of flour
until it worked all through the dough."*

 Activity

SALLY LUNN BREAD – Place water and sugar in a
bowl. Dissolve yeast in the liquid. Watch the
liquid start to bubble. Cream butter in separate
bowl. Add eggs. Add yeast mixture, flour and
sugar. Beat well. Cover batter and let rise till
almost double (about 1 hour). Beat down. Pour
into a bread or tube pan. Let rise again, about 30
minutes, till almost double. Bake at 180°C
(350°F), Gas Mark 4, for 40-45 minutes.

 Why it works

Bubbles show the yeast working. It is actually a
plant that only grows when fed. Sugar feeds the
yeast. The yeast makes 2 products as it grows:
carbon dioxide that causes the dough to rise; and
alcohol that gives off a fermenting smell. The
alcohol cooks off when the bread bakes.

 Talk about it

Yeast is made to work, not just sit. Similarly, we
can let money sit or put it to work. Discuss how
invested money grows and helps other things
grow, like mission work. Why do you think
people sometimes call money – dough
or bread?

DAY 2

BARBECUED PENNIES

LUKE 8:3 *Joanna, the wife of Cuza, the manager of Herod's household, Suzanna, and many others. These women were helping to support them [Jesus and disciples] out of their own means.*

 Activity

Slice hot dogs into ¼ inch pieces. They look like coins. Cook them in barbecue sauce in a pan or in a microwave. Enjoy eating the barbecued pennies.

 Talk about it

Notice how fast the hot dog pieces get eaten up. Do pennies get gobbled up as fast? How quickly does money get spent? Talk about choosing when and how to spend money.

DAY 3

GOD WEIGHS THE MOTIVES

PROVERBS 16:2 *All a man's ways seem innocent to him but motives are weighed by the Lord.*

 Activity

Make piles of ten coins – then remove one coin from each pile. Ask the children which pile is the biggest, which weighs the most, and which one they want.

 Talk about it

God only asks for tithes or a tenth not nine tenths yet all belongs to Him. We need to measure our money and see what to give God. The amount is not important. God doesn't weigh the money instead He weighs motives. Talk about motives and what God wants. Discuss how God weighs our motives.

Masks

Happy is the family that sees behind masks for they will discover hidden qualities.

These activities help children understand the importance of revealing our Christianity.

— MATERIALS —

✧ paper plates or large paper bags
✧ markers and crayons
✧ scissors
✧ paper bag filled with assorted objects (pine cone, spoon, ball, soda can, stuffed animal, etc…)

DAY 1

MAKING MASKS

MATTHEW 10:26 *There is nothing concealed that will not be disclosed, or hidden that will not be made known.*

 Activity

Decorate the plates or bags as masks. Cut out eyes. Put them on or hold them up to cover faces.

 Talk about it

Do we ever hide our feelings behind the mask of a smile? Is this good? Can we hide our thoughts from God? Read *Psalm 139* to find out.

DAY 2

IDENTIFYING HIDDEN OBJECTS

PSALM 139: 23 *Search me O God, and know my heart; test me and know my anxious thoughts.*

 Activity

Let everyone reach in the bag without looking and guess one object they feel. Ask them to describe the color or other specifics about the object. Dump out the contents and see who guessed correctly.

 Talk about it

When we feel with our hands we can identify some things but we may not know everything about an object. When we take them out we discover more, such as the color or smell. When God searches our hearts He sees everything but He can't do anything before we ask for His help. He gave us a free will (complete freedom to make our own decisions) so our fears remain until we let Him help.

DAY 3

FREEZE & WITNESS

EPHESIANS 5:15-16 *Be very careful, then, how you live... making the most of every opportunity, because the days are evil.*

 Activity

This is a type of improvisation. Do this as a group or in pairs. Let one person be a caller. Walk around till someone calls freeze. Everyone freezes in position. Tell one person to start an action. Call out unfreeze. The others unfreeze and start talking to the person doing the motion, seeing if they can bring the talk around to Jesus. Set a time limit if necessary or call out freeze again. Repeat the game.

 Talk about it

We don't know who we will meet in life but we should always be ready to share our love for Jesus and the gospel message. How can we do this?

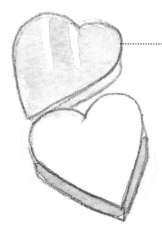
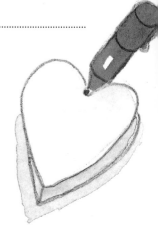

Priorities

*Happy is the family that sets priorities
for they will reach their goals.*

Children will learn that to achieve
goals it takes focus and work.

— MATERIALS —

✧ craft foam (or poster board)
✧ markers
✧ paper and pencils

DAY 1

HEARTS FILLED WITH JOY
(Jesus 1st, others 2nd, yourself last)

MATTHEW 22: 37, 39 *Jesus replied, "Love the Lord
your God with all your heart, and with all your
soul, and with all your mind."... "And the second is
like it, "Love your neighbor as yourself."*

 Activity

Cut out hearts from craft foam. Use markers to
write the words Jesus, Others, and Yourself so
that the first letters go down forming the word
JOY. Place these where you will see them. Add a
magnet and put one on a refrigerator. Glue on
journals or notebooks. Make some for friends
and to use in place of gift bows.

 Talk about it

When we look first to Jesus, secondly to others,
and finally to ourselves, we will discover the
meaning of joy. When we look to Jesus, we look
to eternal life and joy. When we look at others
and their needs, it takes our minds off ourselves.
It's only then that we discover others have
problems and blessings too. How does putting
others ahead of ourselves bring joy?

Jesus
Others
yourself

DAY 2

GOALS

PHILIPPIANS 3:14 *I press on toward the goal to win the prize for which God has called me heavenward in Christ Jesus.*

 Activity

Set up a race course with some obstacles and a finish line. Take turns running to the goal, and applaud each person as they reach the finish line. Reward them with a hug.

 Talk about it

What did it take to reach the goal? Could you do it without moving? How did it feel to reach the goal? Did everyone know which way to run and how to overcome obstacles? Discuss life goals. Talk about obstacles that might be problems and how to overcome the obstacles.

DAY 3

PLANS

JAMES 4:15 *Instead, you ought to say, "If it is the Lord's will, we will live and do this or that."*

 Activity

Have everyone write or draw some goals – one short term goal (something they want to learn or achieve) and one long term goal. Then write down steps needed to reach the goal.

 Talk about it

Let each person describe their goals and let everyone suggest ways to achieve the goals and see if more steps need to be added. Draw little red flags on steps that might be hard as reminders to pray for these steps. Post the goals. Children may want to position these goal lists near where they do their schoolwork.

WEEK FORTY~FIVE

Multiplying Bread & Talents

Happy is the family that knows God multiplies joys for their sorrows will be lessened.

Use theses activities to help children trust in a God who can multiply blessings.

— MATERIALS —

✧ paper
✧ sponges
✧ paint
✧ concentrated cleaner
✧ bucket and water

DAY 1

JESUS AND THE BOY'S BREAD

JOHN 6:9 *Here is a boy with five small barley loaves and two small fish, but how far will they go among so many?*

 Activity

Look at a tiny measure of concentrated cleaner. Does it look like it can clean much? Add it to a bucket of water. Now it will go much farther. Give everyone a rag or sponge and have them clean something.

 Talk about it

Read about Jesus multiplying bread. Talk about how Jesus performed a miracle after a child chose to share what he had. Sharing starts many things into motion. When you share work it gets done faster. Think of what you can share and how that might multiply, such as smiles, pennies, or food.

94

DAY 2

SPONGE PRINTING

JOHN 6:11 *Jesus then took the loaves; gave thanks, and distributed to those who were seated as much as they wanted. He did the same with the fish.*

 Activity

Cut sponges into shapes of a slice of bread and of a fish.

Dip the sponge shapes into paint and press onto the paper to make a painting.

 Talk about it

This activity reminds us of how the bread and fish were multiplied to feed a very large crowd. We may be only one person, but we can tell many people about Jesus, the Bread of Life. What can you give that God can multiply?

Bread was also multiplied in the Old Testament. Read about what happened in *2 Kings 4:42-44.*

DAY 3

SHARING THE BREAD

JOHN 6:12 *When they had all had enough to eat, he said to his disciples, "Gather the pieces that are leftover. Let nothing be wasted."*

 Activity

Have everyone go to their rooms and find something in good condition they no longer need – clothes, toys, or books. Put them in a box and choose a place to donate them.

 Talk about it

Jesus could have kept multiplying bread so why did He want the leftover bread collected? What happens if bread is just left out and never used? How will sharing things you no longer use or need help others?

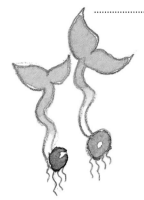

Growing Sprouts

Happy is the family that knows TLC produces a rich harvest for they will sow love.

Watching seeds sprout helps children understand that what they do produces results.

— MATERIALS —

✧ glass jar
✧ cheesecloth
✧ rubber band
✧ seeds for sprouting (alfalfa, bean, wheat, or other quick sprouting seed)
✧ measuring cups
✧ water

DAY 1

PREPARING SEEDS

ISAIAH 58:11 *...You will be like a well-watered garden, like a spring whose waters never fail.*

 Activity

Place ¼ cup of seeds in jar. Cover with one (1) cup of water. Cover opening with cheesecloth secured with rubber band. Let the seeds soak overnight.

 Why it works

A seed is dormant, or sleeping, until it gets water, air, and warmth. Soaking the seed wakes it up. Soaking in water swells the seed and breaks open the shell so it can grow.

Talk about it

How does it feel to be in a bathtub or go swimming? Do you relax? Talk about how a baby grows in a sack of water in the womb. How do Christians open up and grow?

DAY 3

HARVESTING SPROUTS TO EAT

MATTHEW 9:37 *Then he said to his disciples, "The harvest is plentiful, but the workers are few."*

 Activity

After the seeds are a few inches long, place them in sunlight a few hours so they'll turn color. Then enjoy eating them plain, in salad, or in stir-fry.

 Why it works

The sun causes photosynthesis, a type of plant growth that makes the sprouts turn green. They also become more nutritious with sunlight.

 Talk about it

How did the sprouts taste? The sprouts are much bigger than the seeds. When we sow love, it starts a big growth. What should we be sowing?

DAY 2

RINSING AND GROWING

HOSEA 10:12 *Plant the good seeds of righteousness, and you will reap a crop of my love; plow the hard ground of your hearts, for now is the time to seek the Lord, that he may come and shower salvation upon you.* [TLB]

 Activity

Pour off the water, then cover the seeds, add water and pour it off again to rinse the seeds. Place the jar in a warm, dark place, such as in a cabinet. Rinse two times a day. In a day or two the seeds will sprout and start to grow.

 Why it works

The seed is an embryo that contains food. The water causes the plant to digest the food and grow. Rinsing the sprouts cleanses them of gases given off in growth.

 Talk about it

When you're dirty what do you need to get clean? What cleans sin and helps you grow spiritually?

Onward to Victory

Happy is the family that encourages one another for they will be confident.

Encouragement provides support and inspires children to believe they can succeed. Success in small things leads to confidence in other things.

— MATERIALS —

✦ *pennies or other small coins*

DAY 1

BATTLE CRIES — THE WALLS OF JERICHO

JOSHUA 6:20 *When the trumpets sounded, the people shouted, and at the sound of the trumpet, when the people gave a loud shout, the wall collapsed... and they took the city.*

 Activity

Experiment with the power of vibrations. Pile coins on top of a book or on a table. Gently tap around the pile several times then give a hard pound and shout to knock down the pile. Try it on a counter and see how much harder it is to knock down because the counter is a firmer foundation.

 Why it works

Vibrations cause things to fall, such as coins or avalanches of snow or rocks. The power of many voices in union increases vibrations.

 Talk about it

Working together produces results. God used unity instead of military war to win a battle. How has God creatively helped you solve problems?

DAY 2

CREATING CHEERS

EXODUS 15:21 *Miriam sang to them, "Sing to the Lord, for he is highly exalted; The horse and its rider he has hurled into the sea."*

 Activity

Make up a cheer about God or what Jesus has done for your family.

FOR EXAMPLE: Give me a   **J** – *Joy Bringer*

Give me an **E** – *Eternal Life*

Give me a   **S** – *Shepherd*

Give me an **U** – *Uniter*

Give me a   **S** – *Savior*

Who is He – Jesus, Jesus, Jesus... Yeah Jesus!

 Talk about it

Miriam sang her victory song after God saved His people and rescued them from slavery. When God helps you how do you feel? Do you want to shout for joy? A cheer is another way to praise someone and to promote team spirit. Whose team are you on?

DAY 3

VICTORY SONGS

1 CHRONICLES 15:28 *So all Israel brought up the ark of the covenant of the Lord with shouts, with the sounding of rams' horns, and trumpets, and of cymbals, and the playing of lyres and harps.*

 Activity

People paraded with singing and a marching band after they won back the treasured ark of the covenant. Write down all God has done for you. Then sing together a song, such as "I Have Decided to Follow Jesus" or "Oh, Happy Day."

 Talk about it

Talk about the biggest parade you've seen or been in. Why was it fun? Was it a celebration? A parade helps give group spirit as everyone joins in the celebration. Why can we celebrate about God everyday?

The Spice of Life

*Happy is the family that adds spice to
life for they will enjoy variety.*

As children discover the wonderful smell and taste of spices they will understand that Christ adds variety and joy to life.

— MATERIALS —

✧ gingerbread mix
✧ gingerbread cookie cutters
✧ frosting and cookie decorations
✧ thin red licorice for mouths

DAY 1

MAKING GINGERBREAD DOUGH

MATTHEW 5:13 *You are the world's seasoning, to make it tolerable. If you lose your flavor, what will happen to the world? [TLB]*

 Activity

Mix the gingerbread dough. Refrigerate it overnight.

 Talk about it

Mixing the ingredients is only the beginning of making gingerbread cookies. Chilling the dough helps it roll out smoothly. It gives the dough and the cooks time to rest. Correspondingly, as Christians, we need to think about resting, too. Do you have times you need to cool off?

You can smell the spices even as it cooks. Seasonings add zest. How can Christians add spice, or zest, to the world?

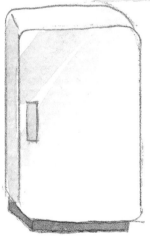

DAY 3

BEING A FRAGRANCE

2 CORINTHIANS 2:14 *But thanks be to God, who always leads us in triumphal procession in Christ, and through us spreads everywhere the fragrance of the knowledge of Him.*

 Activity

Frost and decorate the cookies. Share cookies with friends or neighbors, and enjoy some as a family.

 Talk about it

The cookies smell good because of the spices in them. Spices add zest and flavor to foods. Discuss how the fragrance of Christ changes life? We can give fragrant cookies to others but how can we pass on the fragrance of Christ?

DAY 2

GINGERBREAD CHRISTIANS

PSALM 119:73 *Your hands made me and formed me...*

 Activity

Roll, then cut the dough with cookie cutters, and bake the gingerbread people.

 Talk about it

The dough needs to be pressed and rolled out to be useful. What does God do to make us useful as Christians? Is it an instant process or does it take time like making gingerbread cookies? The oven has to be prepared by preheating it. God prepared for us by sending His son to prepare the way for us. How does God's love help you to love Him more? How does studying God's Word prepare you?

Stretching

Happy is the family that helps children stretch their minds and hearts for they will be united!

Try these activities and discover that families who reach out to God and others will draw close together.

— MATERIALS —

❖ rubber bands
❖ deck of cards
❖ cardboard 2 inches by 6 inches

DAY 1

STRETCHES

PSALM 143:6 *I stretch out my hands to Thee; my soul longs for Thee, as a parched land. [NASB]*

 Activity

Do stretching exercises: Stretch your hands as high as possible and as far out in front as possible. Sit on the floor and stretch your legs straight out in front of you. Stand up and try to touch your toes without bending your knees.

 Talk about it

Stretching makes us limber. Can anyone stretch so far as to do a full split? With practice people can stretch more. Do we stretch our mind? How? How can we stretch out to God? How can we stretch in prayer?

DAY 2

SLING SHOTS AND RUBBER BANDS

1 SAMUEL 17:50 *So David triumphed over the Philistine with a sling and a stone; without a sword in his hand he struck down the Philistine and killed him.*

 Activity

Fold a piece of cardboard one inch at bottom so it will stand up. Draw a giant on the cardboard. Use rubber bands as sling shots to knock down the giant.

 Talk about it

David used a sling as a weapon. A sling can also be used to mend a broken arm. The rubber band in this story was used as a weapon. How else can a rubber band be used? Should it be used as a weapon? What are some Christian weapons?

DAY 3

BINDING TOGETHER

COLOSSIANS 3:14 *And over all these virtues put on love, which binds them all together in perfect unity.*

 Activity

Take rubber bands and stretch them to see how far they can extend. Take a deck of cards and use a rubber band to hold them together tightly. Will one fall out if the deck is dropped or shaken?

 Talk about it

What unites our family? What keeps us close to God? How can more people be united in Christ? Are we willing to stretch ourself and reach out to others and help bind them together in God's family? Think of one way to be a uniter and then make plans so it will happen.

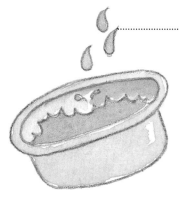

Service With a Smile

Happy is the family that knows children help themselves when they help others for they will learn to serve.

As family members learn to serve one another they feel needed, develop a sense of belonging, and discover the joy of service.

— MATERIALS —

❖ wash basin
❖ towels
❖ foot lotion (optional)
❖ paper
❖ scissors

DAY 1

WASHING FEET

JOHN 13:5 *After that he poured water into a basin and began to wash his disciples' feet, drying them with the towel that was wrapped around him.*

 Activity

Wash and dry the feet of the person next to you. Continue till everyone has their feet washed. If you want, also massage the feet with lotion.

Talk about it

How did it feel to have your feet washed? How did it feel to wash someone else's feet? Is this something you would choose to do if you only had one day left to live? That's what Jesus did. Talk about how we use our feet.

DAY 2

SHARING CHORES – THE GOOD, THE BAD, AND THE DIRTY

GALATIANS 6:2 *Carry each other's burdens, and in this way you will fulfill the law of Christ.*

 Activity and discussion

A special family helps one another – the family you live with and the church family. Write down all the home chores that need to be done. Decide how to divide the work, both the easy chores, like setting the table, and the messier ones, like cleaning toilets. Also think of ways to help at church. Discuss ways to help one another.

List of things to do – Table - John Kitchen Ben Bedrooms Sarah

DAY 3

CIRCLES OF LOVE – REACHING OUT TO OTHERS

1 CORINTHIANS 3:8 *The man who plants and the man who waters have one purpose, and each will be rewarded according to his own labor.*

 Activity

1. Sit in a circle and give the person next to you a smile. Next, give the person next to you a compliment. Repeat this.

2. Fold a circle of paper in half three times, then cut out the heart shape. Open it up and see how the hearts are joined together.

 Talk about it

Is it easier to give a smile or compliment after receiving one? When we lovingly help others or give to others, blessings of love circle back to us. Share times you've helped someone and later received a blessing.

Healing

*Happy is the family that gives their sorrows
to the Lord for they will be comforted*

These activities help children understand God's concern for their feelings and emotional health.

— MATERIALS —

✧ permanent markers
✧ first aid kit or first aid supplies kept in the home
✧ plain bandages, plasters of assorted sizes
✧ rubbing alcohol

DAY 1

COVERING HURTS

LUKE 10:34 *He (Samaritan) went to him and bandaged his wounds, pouring on oil and wine. Then he put the man on his own donkey, took him to an inn, and took care of him.*

 Activity

Look at the family first aid kit. How is each item used? Does it contain everything needed? If not, add the needed items to a grocery store list.

 Talk about it

When you get a small cut and need to stop the bleeding and protect the cut what do you do? (wash it and use a bandages) What size bandages do you use? What if the bandage is not big enough to cover the cut?

When a child is very small, what else helps? (a kiss from their mother). It seems that a little love and care goes a long way to help stop the hurting of a cut for a child! Praise God that His love is big enough to cover all our hurts!

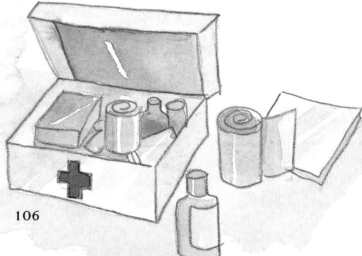

DAY 2

CHRISTIAN BANDAGES

PSALM 147:3 *He heals the brokenhearted and binds up their wounds.*

Activity

Using markers and bandages, let everyone draw designs about God's healing love, such as a heart or a cross on the bandages. Or write verses about healing. Put these healing bandages in the first aid kit. When we have a cut we will remember that Jesus is our healer.

Talk about it

What helps heal us on the inside when our feelings are hurt? Talk about how forgiveness helps people heal.

Extra step

Make and give a package of healing bandages to someone who is recovering now from a hurt.

PRAYER COVERINGS

JAMES 5:14 *Is any one of you sick? He should call the elders of the church to pray over him and anoint him with oil in the name of the Lord.*

Activity

Look at a sticking plaster. Open up the package and examine how it is made.

Talk about it

The plaster must be kept clean and free from germs so it is placed in a sealed package. The soft part covers the cut and the sticky part makes sure it stays in place, protecting the cut. Ointments or salve might also help the wound.

When we are hurt we need to stick close to God and let God protect us. Prayers provide extra salve to help the wound heal.

Some wounds need a doctor. The doctor is like a warrior, fighting sickness and providing skilled protection. Sometimes we need the spiritual care of others – prayer warriors and our pastor.

PSALM 9:9-10 *" The Lord is a refuge for the oppressed, – a place of safety in times of trouble, Those who know you, Lord, will trust in you; You do not abandon anyone who comes to you."*

Planting Seeds in Darkness

*Happy is the family that knows growth
takes time for they will learn patience*

These activities help children develop patience.

— MATERIALS —

✧ seed of a quick growing plant, such as marigold or radishes
✧ soil
✧ flower pot or other container

DAY 1

PLANTING A SEED

JOHN 12:24 *I tell you the truth, unless a kernel of wheat falls to the ground and dies; it remains only a single seed. But if it dies, it produces many seeds.*

 Activity

Plant a seed in a container of good soil. Add a little water.

 Talk about it

The seed will only be a seed until it is planted. In a sense, the seed must die before it can grow. Why is that? How do we grow? Must we die first? How does God help us grow?

108

DAY 2

WATER, MUD, AND GROWTH

1 CORINTHIANS 3:6 *I planted the seed, Apollos watered it, but God made it grow.*

 Activity

Water the seed. Touch the wet soil. Is it sticky?

 Talk about it

Instead of a dry dark place, the seed is in sticky, wet mud. Do you ever feel like you are stuck in mud? The seed needs this water to grow. Jesus tells us in *John 7:37-39*, that we need to believe in Him to receive living water.

DAY 3

GROWTH IN DARKNESS

1 CORINTHIANS 4:5 *Therefore judge nothing before the appointed time; wait till the Lord comes. He will bring to light what is hidden in darkness and will expose the motives of men's hearts. At that time each will receive his praise from God.*

 Activity

Look at the plant. Set the plant in a highly visible location. When it sprouts use it as a centerpiece and talk about how long it took to grow.

 Talk about it

The seed cannot see but still it sprouts roots, and the plant grows up and pops out of the soil. The seed grows toward the warmth from the sun. In like manner, we may not see Jesus, the Son, but we can feel the warmth of His love. Have you felt God's love when you had a problem?

DAY 4

VISIBLE GROWTH

MARK 4:20 *Others, like the seed sown on good soil, hear the word, accept it, and produce a crop — thirty, sixty, or even a hundred times what was sown.*

 Activity

Observe the plant and write down your feelings when it sprouted.

 Talk about it

The plant grows and produces leaves and then a flower or maybe fruit and seeds. New life comes from the seed which was buried.

New fruit can grow in our life, too, but it takes time. Some seeds produce quickly like the marigolds or radishes. Others can take a long time. An avocado tree takes about 5 years to produce an avocado but from then on, it keeps producing many avocados. Each of us grows spiritually at different speeds.

SPECIAL TIMES

Brokenness

Happy is the family that knows failure is a learning experience for they will learn to forgive!

U se activities with eggs to help children understand brokenness.

> — MATERIALS —
>
> ✧ raw eggs
> ✧ bowls
> ✧ spoons

DAY 1

BROKENNESS

ROMANS 3:23 *For all have sinned and fall short of the glory of God.*

 Activity

Plan this devotion for outside. Give everyone a raw egg. Toss the eggs or run races holding the eggs on a spoon until one or more people break their egg.

Talk about it

What stops a person from continuing to participate? Yes, it's because the egg has broken. The shell acts as a protection for the egg – it keeps the inside fresh. Once the egg shell breaks, can the egg be placed back in the shell? Similarly, breaking commandments and doing wrong is easy. How can we be protected from breaking the commandments and doing wrong?

110

DAY 3

OUT OF THE SHELL

ROMANS 8:28 *And we know that in all things God works for the good of those who love him, who have been called according to his purpose.*

 Activity

Think of something to do now for people who might feel broken – the homeless, recent widows, orphans, someone ill or unemployed. Just like cooking, mix in a little comfort for someone else, adding ingredients of love and service. Maybe we should break more eggs and cook something to give someone else?

 Talk about it

What will happen if the egg just sits in the bowl and is not used? Can we use the egg in cooking or eat it if it stays in the shell? Is it good to withdraw into a shell when we feel hurt? How can we draw people out of their shells?

DAY 2

BROKEN EGGS

PSALM 51:17 *The sacrifices of God are a broken spirit; A broken and contrite heart, O God, you will not despise.*

 Activity

Break some eggs in a bowl then discuss what to do with the egg. Cook an omelet or scramble the eggs.

 Talk about it

The egg is not useful to us until it's broken. God needs a broken heart, a heart which knows it's need for God. Let's recall a time when we felt our hearts were broken? Did God use that situation to teach us? What did we learn from it? Did it help us understand other people and their problems?

Victory Celebrations

*Happy is the family that rejoices in the victories
of others for they will learn humility.*

Certificate
for
BEN

Involving children in celebrating
victories of family members helps
them appreciate others and humble
themselves.

--- MATERIALS ---

✦ *yellow poster board*
✦ *scissors*
✦ *decorations: crepe paper streamers,
balloons, or make paper decorations*
✦ *markers*
✦ *colored paper*

DAY 1

I CAN DO IT!

JOHN 21:6 *He [Jesus] said, "Throw your net on the
right hand side of the boat and you will find some."
When they did they were unable to haul the net in
because of the large number of fish.*

 Activity

Let each person name something they worked
hard to learn. Applaud each person's victory. Cut
a trophy from poster board and list the victories.
Display the trophy.

Talk about it

What problems, obstacles, or fears made it hard
to succeed? Did you pray for God's help? How
did God help?

 Talk about it

After David's victory he gave everyone cake and bread. Is it fun to celebrate? Is it fun to pass out a victory dessert to others? Is it fun to share the joy of another person?

DAY 3

LAUREL WREATH

JOHN 12:26 ...*My Father will honor the one who serves me.*

 Activity

Celebrate a victory with a laurel wreath certificate. Make a paper certificate decorated with green leaves. Write down the person's name and accomplishment. You can also weave a crown of silk leaves for the victor.

 Talk about it

Greeks wove wreaths from the evergreen laurel leaf into crowns and placed them on a victor's head to show honor. How does it feel to give honor to someone who worked hard to earn it? How does it feel to be honored? Who does God honor?

DAY 2

CELEBRATE

1 CHRONICLES 16:3 *Then he [David] gave a loaf of bread, a cake of dates and a cake of raisins to each Israelite man and woman.*

 Activity

When someone in the family learns a new skill or succeeds in something, even small victories, celebrate those victories with a special bread, cake, or dessert. Decorate the chair or place of the victor! Let that person serve the dessert. (Ahead of time, determine who you will celebrate during this devotional time.)

Hurt Feelings

Happy is the family that comforts others for they will be loved.

Help children develop compassion through these activities.

— MATERIALS —

✧ ice cubes
✧ 2 plates
✧ poster board
✧ plastic food storage bags and clear tape (or clear contact paper)
✧ markers
✧ clock
✧ calendar

DAY 1

COMPASSION

PSALM 25:16 *Turn to me and be gracious to me, for I am lonely and afflicted.*

 Preparation

Chill one plate and warm one plate.

 Activities

1. Place an ice cube on each plate. Which melts faster?

2. Let each person share a time they felt sad, lonely, or had hurt feelings.

Talk about it

Warmth softens and melts the ice faster than coldness. How can we have warm hearts to melt the coldness that other's feel when they are lonely or sad? Discuss times when you've felt lonely and sad.

DAY 2

MAKE A PLACEMAT

JOHN 14:2 *In my Father's house are many rooms; if it were not so I would have told you. I am going there to prepare a place for you.*

 Activity

Draw names and make a placemat for a family member. Cut the poster board into rectangles just smaller than the bags. Use markers to decorate the poster board with a cheerful face or big heart. Write or draw some of the Beatitudes in *Matthew 5:1-12.* Place the decorated placemats in a bag and seal with tape. (Or cover with clear contact).

 Talk about it

You helped prepare a place for a family member at the table. How does it feel to know God is preparing a room for you in heaven? When you feel lonely look at your placemat and remember that you're important to your family. Remember also that God has a special room set aside for you.

DAY 3

ROOM FOR JESUS

MATTHEW 8:20 *Jesus replied, "Foxes have holes, and birds of the air have nests; but the Son of Man has no place to lay his head."*

 Activity and discussion

1. Take the calendar and fill in upcoming activities and appointments. Look at the clock and talk about what people do at various times of the day. Then ask everyone where does God fit into our time schedule? Discuss.

2. Cut out hearts. Let each person write or draw how they will make room for Jesus every day. Hang them on bedroom doors as daily reminders.

 Talk about it

Do you have family devotions marked on the calendar or do they just get squeezed in once in a while? Do you think it hurts Jesus when we forget Him and leave Him out of our day?

Company

Happy is the family that entertains strangers for they will see God.

Help your children develop hospitality with these activities.

PREPARING FOR COMPANY

ROMANS 16:2 *I ask you to receive her in the Lord in a way worthy of the saints and to give any help she may need from you, for she has been a great help to many people, including me.*

Activity

Invite a new family from church or your neighborhood to dinner or to a picnic. Prepare something special for them, such as a list of the best places in town or the most reliable repair people. If they have young children, make up goodie bags for each child.

Talk about it

Think about what you want to share about your town with the new family and what you want to know about them. Is it fun preparing for people you don't even know?

DAY 2

CELEBRATING

ROMANS 12:13 *Share with God's people who are in need, Practice hospitality.*

 Activity

Plan an international meal. Whether tacos from Mexico or quiche from France, choose foods from a few different countries. Invite guests from different nationalities to come celebrate with you and bring a favorite food, too. You might even make it a church supper!

 Talk about it

Different foods have different flavors and use different spices. Is it fun to try new foods? Would you always like to eat exactly the same meal? How do the differences in people add variety to life?

DAY 3

HEARTS FOR OTHER PEOPLES

MATTHEW 28:19 *Therefore go and make disciples of all nations, baptizing them in the name of the Father and of the Son and of the Holy Spirit.*

 Activity

Try a new food or recipe from another country. Find the country on a map. Look up the people of that country on a map and on the internet.

 Talk about it

How did the food taste? Was it different from what you usually eat? Discuss what you know about the people from the country and their religion. Pray for families in that country.

Traveling With a Road Grab Bag

*Happy is the family that stays close to God
for He will always be with them.*

Taking trips provides opportunities to show children that God is always present, caring for us everywhere.

— MATERIALS —

✧ small bag or container
✧ small objects

DAY 1

MAKE AND FILL THE GRAB BAG!

1 CORINTHIANS 2:9 *However as it is written, "No eye has not seen, no ear has heard, no mind has conceived what God has prepared for those who love Him."*

 Activity

Place several objects into a small container or bag and put it in the family car. Don't reveal the objects. Let others find and place objects in the bag.

 Talk about it

Share how this will be a travel bag to be used in the car when there's a problem or simply boredom. Tell everyone these will be kept secret and only one will be revealed at a time. How does it feel to know surprises are ready for a trip? How does it feel to know God prepares surprises for you, too?

DAY 3

ADDING JOY AS YOU GO

LUKE 12:31 *But seek his kingdom, and these things will be given to you as well.*

 Activity

As you travel add souvenirs to the bag: travel brochures, nature items collected, or items bought as a future surprise.

 Talk about it

When someone discovers a surprise added from a previous trip, discuss some of the memories. Does remembering bring back joyful thoughts? Has God ever added joys to your life? When? How can you add joy to the lives of other people, such as strangers you meet when traveling?

DAY 2

USE IT

PHILIPPIANS 4:12 *I know what it is to be in need, and I know what it is to have plenty. I have learned the secret of being content in any and every situation, whether well fed or hungry, whether living in plenty or want.*

 Activity

The next time everyone is in the car use the travel bag. Let someone reach in and grab an object. Talk about the characteristics of the object and use it to teach about characteristics of people or of God. Objects can include paper clips, pens, a new bag of candy, pennies, cotton balls, or a nail.

 Talk about it

Discuss each object: What is it? How is it useful? Does it have a quality in common with people or God? What can we learn as we look at it. Can we share it, eat it, use it, or give it away?

APPENDIX

Verse	Week	Verse	Week	Verse	Week	Verse	Special
Psalm 139:1-2	1	2 Corinthians 12:9	17	Matthew 21:22	34	Luke 10:34	1
Psalm 139:13-14	1	1 Corinthians 3:16	17	James 4:2-3	34	Psalm 147:3	1
Romans 12:6	1	Acts 1:8	17	Matthew 18:19	34	James 5:14	1
Nehemiah 1:11	2	1 Kings 17:6	18	1 John 1:7	35	John 12:24	2
Mark 7:28	2	Matthew 6:26	18	1 Corinthians 13:12	35	1 Corinthians 3:6	2
Psalm 23:5	2	Matthew 6:33-34	18	Ephesians 5:13	35	1 Corinthians 4:5	2
Matthew 18:20	3	Proverbs 28:20	19	Luke 8:16	36	Mark 4:20	2
Exodus 25:30	3	Psalm 119:2	19	Luke 8:17	36	Romans 3:23	3
Matthew 4:4	3	Hebrews 13:7	19	James 1:17	36	Psalm 51:17	3
Luke 19:4	4	Ephesians 5:15	20	John 14:26	37	Romans 8:28	3
Luke 19:10	4	John 21:9	20	1 Peter 2:21	37	John 21:6	4
1 Peter 3:8	4	1 Corinthians 15:41	20	James 1:5	37	1 Chronicles 16:3	4
Hebrews 13:17	5	1 Corinthians 12:11	21	Ephesians 3:14-15	38	John 12:26	4
Psalm 119:66	5	Colossians 4:6	21	Matthew 7:20	38	Psalm 25:16	5
Philippians 4:8	5	John 3:16	21	Philippians 2:2	38	John 14:2	5
Luke 24:35	6	Luke 21:3	22	1 Peter 4:10	39	Matthew 8:20	5
Acts 2:42	6	Psalm 31:19	22	Romans 12:4	39	Romans 16:2	6
John 6:35	6	2 Corinthians 9:7	22	Ephesians 4:16	39	Romans 12:13	6
Dueteronomy 6:4	7	Colossians 3:16	23	Luke 11:1	40	Matthew 28:19	6
Psalm 99:5	7	Psalm 150:6	23	Luke 11:3	40	1 Corinthians 2:9	7
1 John 1:9	7	Ephesians 5:19	23	Mark 10:16	40	Philippians 4:12	7
1 Thessalonians 5:18	7	Genesis 9:13	24	1 Peter 3:4	41	Luke 12:31	7
1 John 5:14-15	7	Revelation 4:3	24	2 Kings 4:2	41		
John 20:29	8	John 13:34	24	Colossians 3:12	41		
Mark 8:18	8	Matthew 4:2	25	Matthew 13:33	42		
2 Corinthians 5:7	8	Hebrews 13:2	25	Luke 8:3	42		
Exodus 15:2	9	Psalm 127:1	25	Proverbs 16:2	42		
Acts 16:25	9	Matthew 5:15	26	Matthew 10:26	43		
Psalm 33:1	9	Matthew 5:16	26	Psalm 139:23	43		
Matthew 13:34	10	John 1:9	26	Ephesians 5:15-16	43		
Matthew 17:27	10	Matthew 7:8	27	Matthew 22:37,39	44		
2 Corinthians 3:3	10	Acts 17:11	27	Philippians 3:14	44		
Luke 6:38	11	Matthew 7:7	27	James 4:15	44		
Ecclesiastes 11:1	11	Psalm 127:3	28	John 6:9	45		
James 3:5	11	Genesis 1:27	28	John 6:11	45		
John 2:7	12	1 Corinthians 15:45	28	John 6:12	45		
Matthew 11:15	12	Matthew 13:30	29	Isaiah 58:11	46		
Colossians 3:15	12	Matthew 14:29	29	Hosea 10:12	46		
Luke 5:4	13	Matthew 25:32	29	Matthew 9:37	46		
Matthew 4:19	13	Proverbs 27:17	30	Joshua 6:20	47		
John 21:13	13	Hebrews 10:16	30	Exodus 15:21	47		
1 Peter 5:7	14	Ephesians 1:13	30	1 Chronicles 15:28	47		
Psalm 66:18	14	Matthew 3:16-17	31	Matthew 5:13	48		
Matthew 21:22	14	Isaiah 40:26	31	Psalm 119:73	48		
James 4:3	14	Ephesians 3:19	31	2 Corinthians 2:14	48		
Matthew 6:28-29	15	Matthew 7:26	32	Psalm 143:6	49		
Romans 1:20	15	Matthew 7:24-25	32	1 Samuel 17:50	49		
Matthew 25:21	15	Psalm 32:8	32	Colossians 3:14	49		
James 1:22	16	1 Corinthians 14:33	33	John 13:5	50		
Romans 12:2	16	Acts 18:28	33	Galatians 6:2	50		
Acts 2:4	16	Hebrews 11:2	33	1 Corinthians 3:8	50		